THE EMERGENT MANAGER

Field Guide to Your First Six Months as a Manager

Jesse Jacoby
Emergent

The Emergent Manager: Field Guide to Your First Six Months as a Manager

Published by Emergent.

ISBN: 979-8-9972411-0-0 (paperback)

ISBN: 979-8-9972411-1-7 (ebook)

First edition, 2026.

TheEmergentManager.com

Contents

INTRODUCTION

The Job No One Trained You For

On Friday you were one of the best people on your team. On Monday you were responsible for it.

If that shift felt abrupt, you are not imagining it. For most of your career you were rewarded for what you could produce yourself: the quality of your work, your expertise, your reliability. Then, almost overnight, the job changed. Your success is now measured by what other people produce. The very skills that earned you the promotion are no longer the ones the job requires.

Here is the part no one tells you: almost no one is prepared for this. Study after study finds that the large majority of new managers, well over three-quarters, step into the role with no real management training. They are handed a team, a title, and a vague instruction to figure it out. Many do, eventually, through a bruising process of trial and error. A good number never quite recover from a rough start. The failure is rarely a lack of talent. It is the lack of a plan.

That is what this book gives you: a plan.

Management has a simple definition that takes a career to master. It is the art of getting things done through other people. Your technical skills got you in the door. Your people skills, how you set direction, build relationships, earn trust, and move a group toward a goal, will determine how far you go from here. Those skills can be learned. They are not a personality type you either have or lack.

They are a set of moves you can practice, and the first months in the role are when practicing them matters most.

Why focus on the beginning? Because transitions are leverage points. Early on, expectations are still forming, relationships are still fluid, and a small course correction is easy. Wait too long and habits harden, impressions set, and the same correction takes enormous effort. The managers who thrive are not the ones who know everything on day one. They are the ones who move through the transition deliberately instead of being swept along by it.

This book is organized around that transition, in four phases.

Taking Hold is where you land well: clarifying your role, pinpointing what actually matters, and starting without stumbling.

Immersion is where you learn the terrain: yourself, your boss, and how the organization really works beneath the org chart.

Reshaping is where you make your mark: building your team, resolving the tensions that hold it back, and setting a direction people will follow.

Consolidation is where you make it stick: deepening the relationships that sustain you and honestly measuring whether it is working.

Twenty-two short chapters carry you through those four phases, roughly in the order you will need them. Think of each chapter as a single management skill: one focused capability, short enough to read in a sitting and built to be used, not just read. You will find a clear *Outcome* at the start, the core ideas in the middle, and a *This Week* action at the end that turns the reading into something you actually do. Along the way, *Watch out for* boxes flag the traps that most often catch new managers, and *AI on your team* boxes show you how to put an AI assistant to work on that chapter's task. Most chapters point you to a tool (a checklist, worksheet, or template) that does the heavy lifting, and you will find every one of them ready to use in the Toolkit at the back of this book. Together they turn the book from advice into a working system. If you would rather fill them in on a screen, or want the full set laid out as one connected six-month companion, that is what the workbook is for.

A note on who this is for. If you are a brand-new manager, this book is written for you first, and I have tried never to assume you already know the unwritten rules. If you are an experienced manager stepping into a new company, team, or expanded role, the same transition applies; you will simply move through some chapters faster. Either way, treat the timeframes as guides, not rules. Your situation sets the pace. And while the six months in the title is the transition itself, some of what it sets in motion, your objectives, your team, your vision, keeps unfolding across the first year.

This material comes out of twenty years of working alongside managers, from first-time supervisors to senior leaders, at Fortune 500 companies, mid-sized firms, and startups. The patterns are remarkably consistent. The people who struggle and the people who soar are usually separated not by raw ability but by whether they had a plan. Consider this yours.

One last thing before we start. If you feel some anxiety right now, a quiet worry that you might not be ready, that is normal, and it is actually a good sign. It means you take the responsibility seriously. The goal of this book is not to make the worry disappear by pretending the job is easy. It is to replace the worry with a plan, one concrete move at a time.

Let's begin.

PART I: TAKING HOLD (LAND WELL)

CHAPTER 1

Set the Stage Before You Start

Prepare for Your Role

> ◎ **OUTCOME**
>
> By the end of this chapter you will have shaped how you are introduced to the organization, lined up a small personal advisory board, and turned your intentions into a first action plan.

Two managers start on the same Monday. The first sends a breezy note to her new team: thrilled to be here, big changes coming, let's move fast. Within a week the people who admired her predecessor have quietly decided she does not respect what came before, and the colleague who wanted her job has begun collecting allies. The second manager's arrival is announced differently. It thanks the departing leader by name, points to the team's recent wins, and says she is looking forward to learning before she changes anything. Same role, same talent. One spent her first month climbing out of a hole she dug on day one. The other spent it building.

That contrast is the whole point of this chapter. There is a strong pull, in the days before you start, to just get in there and prove yourself. Resist it for a moment. The managers who transition best spend some of their earliest energy not on the work itself but on two quieter things: how they arrive, and who they can lean on. Both are easy to shape before the noise begins. Both are painful to fix later.

Start with a fact that is oddly freeing: you will never feel fully ready. No matter how much you learn beforehand, a great deal only becomes clear once you are in the seat. So the goal of preparation is not to know everything. It is to get right the few things you can control before day one, and to line up the support that will carry you through everything you cannot.

Shape how you are introduced

The way your appointment is announced matters more than it seems. In most organizations people read announcements closely, and they read between the lines: what is said, what is pointedly not said, any hint of changes to come, and how the person you are replacing is treated. A clumsy announcement can create confusion and quiet resistance before you have said a single word.

So do not leave the wording to chance. Work with your boss, and where appropriate HR, to shape it. A good announcement does three things at once. It signals that some change will come, which gives you room to lead rather than boxing you into keeping everything exactly as it was. It honors your predecessor and their contributions rather than disparaging them, because the people who respected that person are watching, and some of them are now yours to lead. And it acknowledges, gently, that you will need others' cooperation to succeed, which invites help instead of assuming it.

See how much a single sentence can carry. A weak version: "Maya is taking over for Hal and will be shaking things up." In eleven words it manages to diminish Hal, alarm everyone who liked how things were, and promise upheaval before Maya understands the work. A stronger version: "Maya joins us to build on the strong foundation Hal leaves behind, and will spend her first weeks listening before proposing where we go next." Same facts, opposite landing. One buys Maya resistance; the other buys her room.

Pay special attention to anyone who wanted your job and did not get it. An internal candidate who was passed over may feel slighted, and how the announcement treats them, and how you approach them in your first weeks, will either lay the groundwork for a working relationship or plant the seed of resistance. You will do the real work of winning them over later, in Chapter 5. It starts here, with an announcement that does not rub salt in the wound.

A special case deserves its own mention: being promoted from within. Often there is no formal announcement at all, just a quiet shift from peer to boss over a weekend. Do not let that pass unmarked. Say something, both to the team and one-on-one to the people who now report to you, especially the friend you used to trade complaints with and the colleague who wanted the role. Naming the change with a little grace is far better than pretending nothing happened while everyone around you privately recalibrates.

One more note for today: your announcement is rarely a single memo anymore. It is also your first email to the team, your introduction in the group chat, and maybe a short video. The principles are identical across every channel. Arrive with warmth, with respect for what came before, and with a light signal of where you hope to go.

> ⚠ **WATCH OUT FOR**
>
> Three easy ways to fumble your entrance: announcing before you and your boss actually agree on the message; promising sweeping change you cannot yet deliver (or promising none, which strands you); and, later, stacking your advisory board with people who will only ever agree with you.

Build your advisory board

Most new managers try to figure everything out on their own. It feels like what a leader is supposed to do. It is also one of the lonelier and riskier ways to run a transition. The managers who do this well quietly assemble a small, personal advisory board: a handful of people whose judgment they trust and can call on when a decision is hard or a situation is unfamiliar.

Think about the perspectives you will need, then find a person for each. Someone who knows the organization's history and politics. A savvy peer who is a step ahead of you. A mentor who has made this kind of leap before. And at least one person who will tell you the truth when you are about to make a mistake. Your predecessor, if they left on good terms, can be one of the most valuable members of all. As you choose, resist the temptation to fill the board with people who simply like you. A board of cheerleaders is worse than no board, because it hands you false confidence exactly when you need candor.

Then, and this is the part people skip, actually ask them. Tell each person plainly that you respect their judgment and would like to be able to come to them as you find your feet. Most will be glad to help, and quietly flattered to be asked. You are not requesting a large commitment. You are building a private board you can consult when the stakes are high and the answer is not obvious.

Turn intentions into a plan

Preparation only pays off if it becomes action. As you move through this book, capture the specific things you decide to do into a simple action plan, starting now, with this chapter: the announcement you want, the people you will invite onto your board, the passed-over colleague you will reach out to. An intention you write down and give a date becomes a commitment. One you leave in your head becomes a regret.

None of this takes long, and all of it compounds. An hour spent shaping your entrance and lining up your board can save you months of undoing a bad first impression. You will spend the rest of this book learning what to do once you are inside. This chapter is about walking in on the front foot.

> **AI ON YOUR TEAM**
>
> Use the days before you start to get smart fast. Ask an AI assistant to brief you on your new organization: recent news, leadership, products, and any public signals about its culture and priorities. Have it help you draft your first note to the team, then ask it to play a skeptical team member and pressure-test how your message might land. You will walk in better prepared, and harder to surprise.

> **THIS WEEK**
>
> 1. Work with your boss and HR on your appointment announcement; make sure it honors your predecessor and signals room to lead.
> 2. List three to five people for your personal advisory board and the perspective each one brings, then ask them.
> 3. Note anyone who was passed over for your role, and how you will approach them in your first weeks.
> 4. Start an action plan and capture your first commitments, each with a date.
>
> **Tools:** *Appointment Communication Plan, Sample Appointment Memo, Personal Advisory Board Worksheet, and Action Plan (in the Toolkit appendix, Chapter 1). Fillable versions are in the companion workbook and free at TheEmergentManager.com.*

PART I: TAKING HOLD (LAND WELL)

CHAPTER 2

Find the Few Things That Matter

Your Key Few Objectives

> ◎ **OUTCOME**
>
> By the end of this chapter you will have named the two or three objectives that will define your success in the coming year, and you will know how to lock them in with your boss so everyone is judging you by the same yardstick.

In his first month as a manager, Marcus said yes to everything. He took on every request, joined every meeting, and stayed later than anyone on the floor, certain the effort would speak for itself. Six months later he was exhausted and, to his genuine surprise, viewed as a disappointment. The trouble was never how hard he worked. It was that he had never stopped to ask which two or three things his boss and the business actually needed from him, so he spread himself thin across everything, including a great deal that did not matter. Effort was the easy part. Marcus brought plenty of it. What he lacked was focus.

That is the trap, and almost every new manager is tempted by it: the quiet assumption that doing more of everything will add up to doing well. It rarely does. A manager's job is not to do the most. It is to make sure the most important things get done, and that requires knowing, with some precision, what the most important things are.

The honeymoon period for new leaders is also shorter than it has ever been. The comfortable grace period managers could once count on has largely evaporated; today you are expected to get it right faster, and false starts are forgiven less easily. In that environment, the most valuable thing you can do in your first weeks is to figure out what right actually means in your particular role, and to figure it out before you have burned your energy on the wrong things.

I call the answer your Key Few Objectives, or KFOs: the two or three critical objectives you must accomplish within your first six to twelve months in order to be judged successful. Not the ten items on your job description. Not everything that lands in your inbox. The key few.

Why few? Because attention is the scarcest resource you have, and it does not divide well. Here is a truth that surprises many new managers: you can successfully accomplish a long list of objectives and still be judged a failure, if the ones you missed were the ones that mattered most. The reverse is also true. Nail the key few, and a surprising amount of forgiveness flows your way on everything else. Focus is not about doing less for its own sake. It is about making sure your best energy lands on the objectives that will actually decide how your first year is remembered.

How to find your Key Few Objectives

Start with what you already know. You almost certainly discussed the priorities of this role during the hiring or promotion process. Before you have another conversation, go back through your notes, the job description, the emails, the things people kept emphasizing when they were selling you on the role. The outline of your KFOs is usually already sitting there in plain sight.

If you come out of that with a list of eight things that all feel important, narrow it with a single question: which two or three, if you nailed them, would most change how your boss and your key stakeholders judge your first year? That is not the same as which are most urgent, or which you happen to be best at. It is which ones your success will actually be measured against. Those are your key few. The rest are context, real work, but not the work you will be remembered for.

Then, and this is the step most people skip, confirm them with the people who will judge you. In an ideal world, everyone you report to would already agree on what your key challenges are. In the real world, false assumptions, conflicting expectations, and the occasional hidden agenda are common. If those disagreements are never surfaced, they do not disappear; they resurface later, as a disappointing review. Your job is to bring them into the light now, while they are still cheap to resolve. Sit down with your boss, and with the other stakeholders whose opinion of you carries weight, and get explicit agreement on your KFOs, stated concretely enough that anyone could tell whether you hit them. "Improve team morale" is a wish. "Cut voluntary turnover on the team from 15 percent to 8 percent by the end of the third quarter" is an objective.

And do not assume. Ask. It is tempting, especially if you were promoted from within, to believe you already know what the job requires. Resist that. The view from the manager's chair is different from the view from the seat you just left, even when the desk is ten feet away. Build your understanding deliberately, by observing, by talking to people who have been here longer, and by reading the material that surrounds the role, and then check that understanding against the people who set your priorities. The gap between what you assume matters and what they say matters is some of the most useful information you will get all year.

> ⚠ **WATCH OUT FOR**
>
> One of the most common reasons capable people struggle in a new management role is that they lean too heavily on the knowledge, skills, and instincts that served them well in the past. The new job almost always calls for new skills and new ways of thinking, and the confidence that got you here can quietly become the blind spot that holds you back. Naming your KFOs honestly means asking not just what you must achieve, but what you will need to learn in order to achieve it.

Lock it in: the Role Charter

Once your KFOs are clear, something useful happens: everything else gets easier to sort. When you know your key tasks, you have a firmer sense of how your performance will be judged, a cleaner basis for saying yes and no, and a clearer picture of what you still need to learn. But a verbal understanding is only a start. Memory drifts, people hear the same conversation differently, and six months is a long time to rely on everyone remembering a hallway chat the same way.

The most reliable way to hold agreement in place is to write it down, and the tool for that is the Role Charter: a short, formal document that forces you, your boss, and your key stakeholders to state clearly what your job is, what it is not, and what will matter most in judging your success. A good Role Charter covers three things.

Your role. Your title, who you report to, what you are accountable for, the scope and boundaries of your authority, and, above all, your Key Few Objectives.

Your relationships. The key stakeholders you will need to work through, inside and outside your team, and what each of them needs from you.

Your development. The skills or knowledge you will need to build to deliver on the role, named honestly rather than glossed over.

Some of this will look obvious, your title, who you report to, until you actually try to write it down and discover that even the basics are fuzzy in a modern organization full of dotted-line reporting and matrixed relationships. That fuzziness is exactly what the Role Charter exists to resolve, and better to resolve it on paper in month one than in a conflict in month five.

The process is straightforward. Draft a first version from your current understanding. Share it with your boss and give them time to react. Sit down together, ideally with an HR partner in the room, to talk it through and reconcile any differences. Then make the agreed revisions and circulate the final version, so everyone is working from the same page, literally. Presenting your boss with a thoughtful draft does something subtle and powerful: it shows you think clearly about priorities, and it shifts the conversation from vague expectation to shared, written commitment.

Finally, turn objectives into action. For each of your key few, sketch more than one way you might get there. Identify the authorities, decisions, people, time, and money each path would require. Test your assumptions against people who have been here longer; ask your team and your peers what has been tried before and how it went. Then bring your recommended plans to your boss, both to confirm you have the authority and the resources you will need and to agree on the preferred path. You will walk out of that conversation with something most new managers never get: a clear, shared definition of what success looks like, and an agreed route to it.

That clarity is the foundation everything else in this book builds on. Get it right and the rest of your transition has a spine to hang everything else on. Skip it, and you risk spending your hardest, best work on objectives that were never the ones that counted.

AI ON YOUR TEAM

Before you meet your boss, try this: give an AI assistant your notes from the hiring process, your job description, and any recent priorities you have been sent, and ask it to name the three objectives that show up most consistently and the two or three that seem to be in tension with each other. It will not decide your Key Few Objectives for you, but it is a fast, honest way to pressure-test whether the key few in your head are really the key few, and to spot the conflicts worth raising before they become surprises.

THIS WEEK

1. Write down what you believe your two or three Key Few Objectives are, in specific, measurable terms.
2. List the people whose judgment of your success matters most, your boss first.
3. Put a 30-minute conversation on the calendar with your boss to confirm your KFOs and surface any differences.
4. Draft a one-page Role Charter using the template in the Toolkit, and bring it to that conversation.

Tools: *Role Charter Template, Role Charter Research Checklist, and a Completed Example (in the Toolkit appendix, Chapter 2). Prefer to type? Fillable versions are in the companion workbook, and a free starter kit is at TheEmergentManager.com.*

PART I: TAKING HOLD (LAND WELL)

CHAPTER 3

Start on the Right Foot

Your first weeks with the team

> ◎ **OUTCOME**
>
> By the end of this chapter you will have a plan for your first team meeting and your early one-on-ones, and you will know how a manager assimilation session can surface what your team really thinks, fast.

On her third day, a new manager gathered her team and walked them through the reorganization she had been designing since before she accepted the job. It was a good plan. It landed like a slap. The team had spent two years building the very thing she was now rearranging, and she had not asked a single one of them a single question. She spent the next six months earning back the ground she gave away in ninety minutes.

First impressions are stubborn. The read your team takes of you in your first weeks will color how they hear everything you say for months afterward. And here is the counterintuitive part: the fastest way to earn their confidence is not to show them how much you know about the work. It is to show them how much you value them. For the first few weeks, put relationships ahead of results.

That does not mean going soft on the work. It means signaling, in what you do and not just what you say, that you understand a simple truth: your success now runs entirely through other people. It depends on the effort of each individual on your team, and on how well they pull together. When your actions make clear that you know this, you begin building the trust and commitment you will need to get anything done.

Hold your first meetings

Meet your whole team quickly, ideally within your first day or two. Resist the urge to arrive with a plan. Your first team meeting is not the place to unveil a vision; you do not yet have one worth sharing, and you have not earned the standing to impose it. It is the place to show up as a person, to say plainly that you know the team's success depends on them, to acknowledge the work they have already done, and to begin listening. Tell them what they can expect from you in these early weeks: that you intend to learn before you change anything.

Then meet each of your direct reports one-on-one, within the first week or two. Come with questions rather than answers. What are you working on? What is going well? What gets in your way? What do you wish the last manager had done differently? What do you need from me? Ask, and then mostly listen. These conversations are not for making decisions. They are for building the map you will use to make good ones later.

If your team is spread across locations, hold these first conversations individually and by video rather than in one group call, and start with the people furthest from you. The person you will meet last is usually the person who most needs to know you noticed them, and first impressions travel more slowly across a distance. Chapter 19 goes into what changes when you rarely share a room.

> ⚠ **WATCH OUT FOR**
>
> Two traps in these early conversations. First, do not make promises. Someone will raise a real problem and you will want to fix it on the spot, but a commitment you cannot keep costs you far more than the goodwill of making it. Say you have heard them, that you will look into it, and then actually do. Second, do not pick favorites, or even appear to. In your first weeks everyone is quietly watching who you lean toward, and early impressions of favoritism are hard to undo.

Consider a manager assimilation meeting

For a faster and deeper read, especially if you have inherited a team that carries some history, consider a manager assimilation meeting. It is a structured, facilitated session, usually run by someone from HR, designed to compress weeks of guarded getting-to-know-you into a single afternoon. It works in three moves.

First, your team meets without you, with the facilitator, and is invited to say what it really thinks, anonymously: their hopes for the team, their worries, and the questions they have about you and where things are headed. The facilitator records all of it. Second, you and the facilitator sit down so you can hear it, unfiltered, and prepare. Third, you rejoin the team and respond, working through their questions and concerns openly, and together you turn the biggest issues into a short action plan.

The power is in the anonymity. People will put on the table things they would never say to a new boss's face in week one, and they will say them now, while the issues are still small and cheap to address, rather than six months from now after they have hardened into resentment. The session also does the reverse: it gives you a natural platform to convey your expectations and to address, in one honest conversation, concerns that might otherwise have simmered for a quarter. It works just as well over video, which matters if your team is spread across locations.

Then follow through

However well your first meetings go, they are a promise, not proof. Your team will decide what to make of you not by what you said in the room but by what you do in the weeks after it. Keep the conversations going; check back in over the next few months to learn how people's views are shifting; and if you ran an assimilation session, hold a short follow-up to show the team you acted on what you heard.

Nothing builds trust in a new manager faster than being someone who listens and then visibly does something about it. The smallest kept commitment in your first month, the thing you said you would fix and quietly fixed, is worth more than the finest opening speech. Start there, and the harder work of the chapters ahead has solid ground to stand on.

> **AI ON YOUR TEAM**
>
> Let AI handle the prep so you can be present in the room. Ask it to draft talking points for your first team meeting and a tailored set of one-on-one questions for each report based on their role. Afterward, feed it your (anonymized) notes from all the conversations and ask what themes repeat across the team. It will not build the relationships for you, but it will help you spot the pattern you might miss when you are meeting ten people in a week.

THIS WEEK

1. Schedule and hold a whole-team meeting in your first days. Come to listen and set the tone, not to unveil plans.
2. Book a one-on-one with each direct report for week one or two, and ask more than you tell.
3. Ask HR whether a manager assimilation session makes sense for your team.
4. Pick one or two small commitments you can make good on quickly, then deliver them.

Tools: *Meeting Navigation Guide and Manager Assimilation Meeting Guide (in the Toolkit appendix, Chapter 3). Fillable versions are in the companion workbook and free at TheEmergentManager.com.*

PART I: TAKING HOLD (LAND WELL)

CHAPTER 4

Map the People Who Matter

The relationships that get work done

> **◎ OUTCOME**
>
> By the end of this chapter you will have identified the handful of people who can make or break your objectives, and you will have the start of a plan to build each of those relationships on purpose.

Six weeks in, a new manager had done everything the books tell you to do. He had aligned with his boss, named his priorities, and run good meetings with his team. Then a project he needed ground to a halt, because the head of another department, someone he had never bothered to meet, quietly moved his request to the back of her queue. It was not personal. He simply was not on her radar, and she was not on his. The most important month of his transition depended on a relationship he had not thought to build.

Work, in a modern organization, gets done through relationships. That has always been somewhat true, but it is truer now than ever. The old command-and-control structure, where you told the people below you what to do and that was the end of it, has been flattened and rewired into something closer to a web. Most of what you need to accomplish sits outside your direct authority, in the hands of people you have to influence rather than instruct. That makes the ability to find and win over the right people one of the most valuable skills you have.

A stakeholder is anyone who has a stake in your work or its outcome, anyone who shares, or might one day share, one of your goals. Some are obvious: your boss, your team. Many are not: a peer whose group you depend on, the finance partner who controls your budget, a customer, a vendor, someone two levels down whose cooperation quietly decides whether your plans move. For each one there are really two relationships to tend, the personal one between you and them, and the working one between your group and theirs. Both matter, and they are not the same.

> ⚠ **WATCH OUT FOR**
>
> The most common stakeholder mistake is to cultivate only upward and inward, pouring your relationship energy into your boss, senior leaders, and your own team while neglecting the peers beside you and the people across and below you. Those are precisely the relationships that blindside new managers. No leader can afford to ignore them. Map the whole web, not just the flattering top of it.

See them clearly

Build your map on observation and judgment, not assumption. It is easy to inherit opinions about people, that this one is difficult, that one is a lightweight, and just as easy to be wrong. Start instead from your Key Few Objectives, the priorities you named in Chapter 2, and ask a sharper question: which relationships must I create, strengthen, or repair in order to achieve these? That turns a vague sense of office politics into a short, focused list.

Some of the people on that list will not think of themselves as your stakeholders at all, at least not yet. Part of your job is to see the connection before they do, and to bring them in. For each person, get concrete: what are their priorities, where do their interests align with yours or collide with them, how much do they actually affect your success, and what is the current state of the relationship, strong, neutral, strained, or not yet built?

Be especially deliberate about the stakeholders you will never bump into. In a shared building, some relationships maintain themselves through sheer proximity. Anyone outside your location has to be scheduled or they will quietly fall off the map, and you will not notice until you need them.

Build the relationships on purpose

You cannot invest equally in everyone, so choose. Identify the handful of relationships that matter most and address those first. Then do the thing most managers skip: go and talk to them. Prepare a few good questions and interview your key stakeholders, not to pitch your agenda but to understand theirs. What are they trying to achieve? What pressure are they under? What would make their working life easier? The fastest way to build a relationship is to understand what the other person cares about and to connect your goals to theirs.

Make every conversation produce something. Turn what you learn into specific action items, a follow-up, an offer of help, a small commitment kept, and fold them into your plan. Relationships are built by investment made before you need anything, so that when you do need something, the account is not empty.

Follow up, and keep a plan

After each conversation, take notes while they are fresh: this stakeholder's priorities, their concerns, where you might help each other.

Check your read against your boss, who has known these people longer than you have and can correct your first impressions. Bring your team in too, they often hold relationships and insight you lack. And keep watching, because relationships drift; part of your job is to notice when one needs attention or repair before it becomes a problem.

Then write it down. A stakeholder plan, even a single page, turns all of this from something that happens by accident into something you do on purpose. It names who matters, the state of each relationship, and your next move for each one. It is the difference between hoping the right people are with you and knowing where you stand. You will lean on this map for the rest of your transition: the vision you set later, the changes you make, the support you need when something goes wrong, all of it travels along the relationships you build now.

> **AI ON YOUR TEAM**
>
> Ask an AI assistant to help you build and maintain your stakeholder map: list everyone connected to your Key Few Objectives, then sort them by how much they influence your work and how supportive they are today. Have it draft tailored questions for each conversation. Afterward, give it your notes and ask it to summarize each person's priorities and flag where two stakeholders' goals collide. You still do the relating; it keeps the map current.

THIS WEEK

1. List everyone with a stake in your Key Few Objectives, up, down, across, and outside. Do not skip the peers beside you.
2. Mark the handful who most affect your success, and the current state of each relationship: strong, neutral, strained, or not yet built.
3. Book a conversation with your top two or three, and go to understand their priorities, not to pitch yours.
4. Start a one-page stakeholder plan, with a next action for each key relationship.

Tools: *Stakeholder Analysis Checklist and Worksheet, Stakeholder Relationship Research Checklist, and Stakeholder Relationship Plan (in the Toolkit appendix, Chapter 4). Fillable versions are in the companion workbook and free at TheEmergentManager.com.*

PART I: TAKING HOLD (LAND WELL)

CHAPTER 5

See Resistance Coming

Turning resistance into cooperation

> ◎ **OUTCOME**
>
> By the end of this chapter you will recognize the forms resistance takes, know how to approach a colleague who was passed over for your role, and have a calm, listening-first way to turn a resister into a contributor.

In her second week, a new manager proposed a small change to how the team logged its work. Everyone in the room nodded. It sounded sensible, and no one objected. A month later, nothing had changed. The old system was still humming along, and when she asked why, she got shrugs and good reasons and more nodding. She had not been argued with. She had been quietly, politely ignored. That is what resistance usually looks like, and it is why the managers who miss it are the ones who mistake a nod for a yes.

Some resistance is close to guaranteed when a new manager arrives, and it helps to expect it rather than take it personally. It tends to come from a few predictable places: someone who wanted your job and did not get it, someone with a genuinely difficult working style, or someone who is simply anxious about the change you represent. Often it is none of those exactly, just the ordinary friction of people adjusting to a new person with new ideas.

What helps most is knowing the shapes resistance takes, because most of it is quiet. It shows up in four recognizable forms. Someone goes silent and stops keeping you in the loop, a lack of communication. Someone drags their feet on the things you are trying to move, a lack of support. Someone becomes reliably critical of you and your ideas. Or someone agrees to do a thing and then simply does not do it, the passive-aggressive yes that goes nowhere. Name these early and you can respond while the problem is still small.

The person who wanted your job

Start with the most predictable resister of all: the internal candidate who wanted your role. Before you assume anything about anyone, talk to your boss. Ask who the likely resisters are, including anyone who was passed over, and ask for their read on how to approach each one. Then meet each passed-over colleague as soon as you can, ideally in your first weeks, before resentment has time to harden.

If they are staying, be sincere. Tell them you know their value, that you are counting on them, and that you are committed to their growth. A genuine career conversation, about where they want to go and how you can help them get there, does more to defuse resentment than any amount of careful diplomacy. If you already know they are leaving, be candid and empathetic. You lose nothing by treating them well on the way out, and the rest of the team notices how you do it.

When resistance shows up, listen first

For every other kind of resister, the move is the same, and it is not the one most new managers reach for. When a roadblock starts to cause real problems, resist the urge to correct or confront. Have a conversation, and lead with listening.

It goes roughly like this. Name the specific roadblock you have observed, without criticizing the person. Ask how they see the situation. Invite them to share what is actually bothering them and what they would want done differently. Only then offer your own perspective, describing the impact of the behavior rather than judging the character behind it. Be clear about the positive behavior you need and what you expect. And close by telling them, and meaning it, that you want them on the team and value what they bring.

The order is the point. Resistance is usually a natural response to the stress of change, and people who feel understood are far more likely to move than people who feel managed. Understand first, correct second.

When it doesn't stop

Listening first is not the same as tolerating anything. If resistance becomes habitual and starts to hurt the person's performance or the team's, the conversation has to change. Bring in HR, learn your organization's positive-discipline process, and give the person every reasonable chance to adopt a more constructive approach. But do not let it drift. Somewhere around eight to ten months in, you need to make a decision, because the cost of an unresolved resister is not only their own output. It is what the rest of your team learns about what you will tolerate. Being kind and being endlessly patient are not the same thing, and your team can tell the difference.

⚠ **WATCH OUT FOR**

Two ways new managers get resistance wrong. The first is missing it, mistaking a room full of nods for agreement while the real objections go underground. The second is overreacting, coming down hard on a resister before you understand what is driving them, which usually deepens the very resistance you were trying to end. Watch for the quiet forms, and lead with curiosity before consequences.

AI ON YOUR TEAM

Before a hard conversation, use an AI assistant to rehearse. Ask it to play the resistant team member, including the defensive version, so you can practice staying calm and curious. Have it help you rewrite judgmental feedback ("you're not on board") into descriptive feedback ("the project has stalled twice after we agreed to move it"). And ask what a person in that spot might actually be worried about. It rehearses; you have the real conversation.

THIS WEEK

1. Ask your boss who the likely resisters are, including anyone passed over for your role.
2. Meet each passed-over colleague in your first weeks; acknowledge their value and commit to their growth.
3. When you spot foot-dragging or a yes that goes nowhere, open a listening-first conversation early, not an accusation.
4. If resistance is habitual and hurting the team, loop in HR and start the clock; do not let it drift past eight to ten months.

Tool: *Understanding Resistance Checklist (in the Toolkit appendix, Chapter 5). Fillable versions are in the companion workbook and free at TheEmergentManager.com.*

PART I: TAKING HOLD (LAND WELL)

CHAPTER 6

Earn Credibility Fast

Trust is the cornerstone

> ◎ **OUTCOME**
>
> By the end of this chapter you will understand what credibility is actually made of, and you will have five concrete ways to build it, starting with an early, visible win.

Picture the most brilliant person you have worked with, the one who always had the answer. Now ask yourself: did the room actually trust them? Often the honest answer is no. Brilliance and credibility are not the same thing, and mistaking one for the other is a quiet way that capable new managers stall. You do not earn credibility by being the smartest person in the room. You earn it by being the most reliable one.

It helps to be precise about what credibility actually is. A useful definition: credibility equals trustworthiness plus expertise. Expertise is what you know and can do, and if you have just been promoted, you probably have plenty. Here is the disconcerting part, and people who have studied this have found it to hold up: trustworthiness tends to carry at least as much weight as expertise, and often more. Most of us climb into leadership by pouring ourselves into our expertise. It turns out that is only half the equation, and not the half people weigh most heavily.

So it is worth understanding trustworthiness, which breaks into four qualities, and the encouraging thing is that all four are within your control. Consistency: your actions match your words, and you keep your commitments. Shared perspective: people extend trust to those who seem to see the world as they do. Frequency of interaction: within reason, the more people deal with you, the more they trust you. And behavioral appropriateness: behaving in ways that fit what the people around you expect. None of these require genius. Every one of them requires discipline.

At a distance, credibility is built almost entirely out of visible reliability. People who cannot see you work can only see whether you do what you said you would do, by when you said you would do it, so responsiveness and follow-through carry weight far out of proportion to how impressive they feel.

Five ways to build it fast

First, keep every commitment. This is consistency, and it is the bedrock of the whole thing. Before you agree to attend a meeting, return a call, or hit a deadline, pause long enough to be sure you actually will. The instinct to please with a quick yes is exactly what gets new managers into trouble, because a small broken promise erodes trust faster than a big win builds it. Under-promise and over-deliver. In your first months, a reputation for doing precisely what you said you would do is worth more than any display of brilliance.

Second, find common ground. Make it a small discipline to find several things you genuinely share with every person you meet, in their background, their interests, or the problems they are wrestling with. This is not manipulation. Shared perspective is one of the oldest foundations of trust, and looking for it makes you a better listener besides.

Third, show up often. Within reason, trust grows with contact. The manager who hides behind email and appears only to hand down decisions stays a stranger. Seek out the people who matter to your success and give them regular, low-stakes contact, not just the high-stakes kind.

Fourth, read the local norms. Credibility lives in the eye of the beholder, so learn what appropriate looks like here. You might prefer a quick hallway update, but if this culture expects a prepared briefing, give the briefing. When in Rome. Matching the expected style is not phoniness; it is respect for the people whose trust you are trying to earn.

Fifth, secure an early win. Look at your Key Few Objectives and find one visible piece you can deliver soon and that will have a positive, organization-wide impact. Nothing builds a new manager's credibility faster than a concrete result people can see. It does not have to be big. It has to be real, and it has to be early.

The cornerstone of everything ahead

Credibility is the foundation your first months rest on, and the reassuring truth is that it is built by discipline, not charisma. Keep your word, find common ground, stay present, fit the room, and put a visible win on the board. Do that, and you close the hardest stretch of any transition holding the one asset that makes everything after it easier: a team and an organization that have decided you are worth trusting.

That completes Taking Hold. You have prepared your entry, pinpointed what matters most, started well with your team, mapped the people who matter, met resistance with a level head, and begun to earn real credibility. The foundation is set. From here the work turns both inward and outward, to understanding yourself and the organization you have joined, which is where the next part begins.

⚠ WATCH OUT FOR

Two credibility traps catch capable managers. The first is leaning on expertise: being the smartest, least-trusted person in the room, and wondering why your good ideas do not land. The second is over-promising to be liked. Every small commitment you drop, the callback you forgot, the deadline you let slip, costs you more trust than you gained by saying yes. Guard your word carefully; in your first months it is the currency you spend and earn.

AI ON YOUR TEAM

Use an AI assistant to protect your consistency and speed your prep. Have it keep a running list of the commitments you make, so none quietly slips. Before a meeting, ask it to surface a few things you might genuinely share with the person, based on their public background. And point it at your Key Few Objectives to brainstorm candidate early wins. It helps you keep your word and find common ground; earning the trust is still yours to do.

THIS WEEK

1. Write down every commitment you have made in your first weeks, and make sure each one is kept.
2. Before your next few meetings, find several things you genuinely share with each person.
3. Learn what "appropriate" looks like here, a briefing or a hallway chat, and match it.
4. Pick one visible early win tied to a Key Few Objective, and go deliver it.

Tool: *Credibility Research Checklist (in the Toolkit appendix, Chapter 6). Fillable versions are in the companion workbook and free at TheEmergentManager.com.*

PART II: IMMERSION (LEARN THE TERRAIN)

CHAPTER 7

Understand How Change Works

Leading your team through it

> ◎ **OUTCOME**
>
> By the end of this chapter you will see change as a process you can work with rather than weather, and you will have five moves for helping your team through it, starting with yourself.

The email went out at 4:58 on a Friday: effective Monday, the team would be reorganized. No why, no context, just the new boxes and lines. By the time the manager arrived on Monday, half the team had spent the weekend polishing their resumes. The change itself might have been the right call. The way it landed turned it into a threat. Managing change is less about the change and more about the people moving through it.

You have taken hold. Now you go deeper, and one of the first realities you will meet is change. Like it or not, part of your job now is to be a change agent. Organizations are always in motion, and new managers in particular often arrive precisely because something needs to shift. Whether the change is yours or handed down from above, your team will look to you to make sense of it. Doing that well comes down to three tasks: helping people understand what is changing and why, building real commitment to where you are headed, and easing the resistance that any change stirs up.

None of it starts with your team. It starts with you.

Get yourself comfortable first

You cannot lead people through a change you have not made peace with yourself. Before you say a word to your team, address your own questions. Talk to your boss, your peers, and anyone who understands the reasoning, until you can explain the change, and believe in it, in your own words. If you have real doubts, this is the moment to raise them, upward and in private. Once you are standing in front of your team, your job is to lead, and a manager who is visibly unconvinced makes everyone else nervous.

It also helps to hold a steadier view of change itself. Change is not an aberration; it is an organic part of how any organization lives and grows. When you treat the confusion and discomfort people feel as a normal part of the process rather than a sign that something has gone wrong, you can meet it with calm instead of adding to the alarm.

Bring your team along

Then talk to your team, as a group and one by one, and give them as much information as you can, as early as you can. In the absence of information, people invent their own, and what they invent is almost always worse than the truth. Be honest about how the change affects them, their work, their roles, their worries, rather than papering over it.

And anchor the whole thing in the future. The surest way to get people on board with a hard change is to be clear and specific about the better place it leads to. People will absorb a remarkable amount of disruption if they believe it adds up to something worth having. Vague reassurance moves no one; a concrete picture of the improvement does.

Set them up to succeed

Understanding and buy-in are not enough if people are not equipped. Ask your team directly what they need to succeed with the change. New skills? Clearer direction? Different tools, more time, or cover from above? Then go and get it. Nothing kills a change faster than asking people to do something new without giving them what it takes to do it, and few things build your credibility faster than clearing those obstacles out of their way.

Then keep at it

Finally, remember that change is not an announcement; it is a process, and processes have an ebb and flow. Enthusiasm dips, old habits reassert themselves, and the news you delivered last month is already going stale. So keep pace with it. Watch how the change is landing on people over time, adjust as you learn, and keep talking about it long after you think you have said it enough. Look for the signs that it is taking hold, that people are folding the new way into how they actually work, and when you see them, name them. What gets noticed gets repeated.

Change is the water a manager swims in, and learning to move people through it well is one of the things that separates managers who merely hold on from those who genuinely lead. It also teaches you the organization. Nothing reveals how a place really works, who holds influence, and what people fear, faster than watching it try to change. Which makes this a fitting place to begin the deeper work of the chapters ahead: learning the terrain you have joined, starting with yourself.

⚠ WATCH OUT FOR

Two ways change goes wrong under a new manager. The first is delivering it as a decree, the new structure without the why, which reads as a threat and breeds the very resistance you then have to fight. The second is announcing it once and assuming the work is done. Change that is not tended slides quietly backward. Say the why, and say it more than once.

AI ON YOUR TEAM

Use an AI assistant to sharpen your case for change. Ask it to help you put the why and the future state into plain language, then to anticipate the questions and objections your team is likely to raise, so none catch you flat-footed. You can also have it draft a simple change-communication plan: what to say, to whom, and when. It helps you prepare the message; the conviction has to be yours.

THIS WEEK

1. Get clear on the change yourself: talk to your boss and peers until you can explain the why and mean it.
2. Tell your team early and fully, as a group and one on one, and connect the change to a concrete better future.
3. Ask each person what they need to succeed with the change, then go remove those obstacles.
4. Set a reminder to revisit the change in a few weeks; watch how it is landing and keep talking about it.

Tool: *Supporting Change Research Checklist (in the Toolkit appendix, Chapter 7). Fillable versions are in the companion workbook and free at TheEmergentManager.com.*

PART II: IMMERSION (LEARN THE TERRAIN)

CHAPTER 8

Know Yourself

The gap between how you see yourself and how others do

> ◎ **OUTCOME**
>
> By the end of this chapter you will have an honest read on your strengths, your blind spots, and the gap between who you are now and who the role needs you to become, plus a way to keep that picture accurate over time.

Ask a room of managers to rate themselves as listeners, and nearly all of them land above average. Ask their teams, and the numbers look very different. That gap, the one you cannot see from inside your own head, is usually the thing that trips you up. You do not get derailed by the weaknesses you already know about. You get derailed by the ones everyone else can see and you cannot.

Self-awareness is one of the most reliable predictors of leadership success, for a simple reason: no one is equally strong at everything, and the leaders who know precisely where they are strong and where they are not can deploy themselves accordingly. Two things are worth finding as you settle into the role. First, the strengths and behaviors you will need to build to hit your objectives. Second, and more important, the blind spots that could quietly hinder or even derail you. The first you can usually feel. The second, almost by definition, you cannot, which is why real self-awareness takes more than introspection.

Three views of yourself

An honest picture of yourself comes from three angles, not one. The first is how you see yourself now. Useful, but limited, because we are all unreliable narrators of our own behavior. The second is how others see you, the view you cannot get from the inside and the one that actually shapes your reputation and your effectiveness. What your team experiences of you is, for all practical purposes, who you are to them. The third is who you want to become, the version of yourself the role requires.

Two gaps then matter. The gap between how you see yourself and how others see you reveals your blind spots. The gap between who you are now and who you want to be is your development agenda. A structured self-assessment, rating yourself across areas like communication, leading and developing others, planning, emotional maturity, and self-knowledge, then having others rate you on the same, turns a vague sense of how am I doing into something specific enough to act on.

Getting the truth from others

Here is the difficulty: almost no one will volunteer honest criticism to a new manager, especially one who now holds sway over their raise and their workload. Ask simply, "any feedback for me?" and you will hear "you're doing great." So make honesty easy and safe. Ask narrow questions instead of open ones: what is one thing I should keep doing, and one thing I should change? Ask about specific situations rather than your character. Where you can, gather input anonymously; the manager assimilation session from Chapter 3 is one good vehicle. And when someone does hand you something hard to hear, your only job in that moment is to thank them. The fastest way to never receive honest feedback again is to argue with the first person brave enough to offer it.

Mind the two gaps

Once you have the three views, do not just study them. Where your self-rating and others' ratings diverge, resist the urge to decide that you are right and they are wrong. That gap is not an insult; it is information, and it points at the exact place your good intentions are not landing the way you assume. Where your current self and your desired self diverge, you have a development agenda, but do not try to fix all of it at once. Pick one or two areas that matter most for your objectives and work on those. Self-awareness without action is just a more sophisticated form of worry.

Finally, treat this as a habit, not an event. The managers who keep growing are the ones who keep a channel open to how they are actually landing, long after the first assessment is filed away. Knowing yourself clearly makes everything in the chapters ahead easier: it is far simpler to play to your strengths, read your boss, and adapt to a new culture once you have an honest sense of what you bring and what you need to watch. The clearer your mirror, the better your judgment.

> ⚠ **WATCH OUT FOR**
>
> Two traps. The first is assuming your self-image is accurate; the most confidently self-assured people are often the least self-aware, precisely because they never check. The second is asking for feedback and then getting defensive when you receive it, which quietly teaches everyone around you to stop telling you the truth. Ask, listen, thank, and only later decide what to do with it.

AI ON YOUR TEAM

Use an AI assistant to turn assessment into action. Feed it your self-ratings alongside the anonymized themes from others' feedback and ask where the gaps cluster and what they might have in common. Have it suggest specific, observable behavior changes rather than vague resolutions. And ask it to help you word the narrow, non-threatening questions that actually draw out honest input. It can organize the mirror; the honesty is still yours to seek.

THIS WEEK

1. Rate yourself honestly on the success factors: which factors are most, and least, descriptive of you?
2. Ask three or four trusted people to rate you on the same factors, or simply for one thing to keep and one to change.
3. Note the biggest gap between how you see yourself and how others see you, and treat it as information.
4. Pick one or two areas to develop toward your desired self, and start.

Tool: *Success Factors Evaluation: Current Self, Others' Ratings, and Desired Self (in the Toolkit appendix, Chapter 8). Fillable versions are in the companion workbook and free at TheEmergent-Manager.com.*

PART II: IMMERSION (LEARN THE TERRAIN)

CHAPTER 9

Play to Your Strengths

And watch their shadow side

> ◎ **OUTCOME**
>
> By the end of this chapter you will know how to lead from your genuine strengths while catching the moments those same strengths, overused, could quietly derail you.

The very quality that earned you this job can be the one that undoes you in it. The meticulous engineer promoted for catching every flaw becomes the manager who cannot stop correcting other people's work. The decisive closer rewarded for fast calls becomes the boss who steamrolls the room and stops hearing dissent. Nothing changed about the strength. The context changed, and a strength that is not watched has a way of curdling into the very thing that trips you up.

Picture your career as a train moving fast down the track. Most of the time everything runs smoothly and you are getting where you mean to go. But trains derail, and so do careers, usually not from some obvious incompetence but from a blind spot or a knee-jerk reaction, a pattern of behavior that works fine in ordinary moments and quietly wrecks the important ones. These patterns have a name: derailers. And here is the uncomfortable truth about them, one that catches most capable people off guard: your derailers are very often just your strengths, overused.

Lead from your strengths

Start with the good news. You were promoted for real reasons, and the fastest way to add value in a new role is to deploy the strengths that got you there deliberately, rather than by accident. Get clear on what this role actually demands, then map your genuine strengths against it. Which matter most here? Which should you lean on hard in the first months? A manager who plays to a real strength, whether it is sharp analysis, or building relationships, or the ability to decide and move, is far more effective than one who spreads thin trying to be adequate at everything.

Watch the shadow side

Now the harder part. Every strength casts a shadow, and in a new and bigger role the shadow grows longer. The analytic thinker slides into analysis paralysis. The decisive leader is seen as impulsive or dictatorial. The person with exacting standards becomes the boss who never fills a position and never says good enough. The confident high performer, coasting on a strong track record, grows arrogant and underestimates a challenge that is genuinely new. In each case the strength did not vanish; it was overused, or used in a situation that called for its opposite. Part of leading yourself well is knowing which of your strengths is most likely to tip over, and catching it before others do.

Know the common derailers

Beyond overused strengths, there is a well-mapped set of behaviors that reliably send careers off the tracks, especially under pressure: arrogance, defensiveness when receiving feedback, insensitivity to the impact you have on others, unreliability on commitments, overmanaging instead of empowering, failing to build a real team. What they share is that they are usually invisible to the person doing them and painfully visible to everyone else, which is exactly what makes them dangerous. This is where the self-awareness work of the last chapter pays off. The honest feedback you gathered there is the surest way to catch a derailer while it is still a habit and not yet a reputation.

Turn it into a plan

Do two things with all of this. First, run a short personal audit. Look back at the roles and relationships that have gone well and the ones that have not, find the pattern, and name the strengths and blind spots behind each. Then ask the sharp question: which of my strengths is most likely to derail me if I overuse it here? Second, choose a small number of deliberate adjustments, strengths to lean into and one or two behaviors to keep on a short leash, and fold them into the same action plan you have been building since Chapter 1. Managing your strengths is not about blunting them. It is about aiming them.

The managers who last are not the ones without weaknesses. They are the ones who know their own edges well enough to use their strengths on purpose and to catch the shadow before it catches them. Do that, and the very traits that got you here will keep carrying you forward instead of quietly working against you.

⚠ **WATCH OUT FOR**

The danger of a strength is that it feels like a virtue right up until it does damage. The high standards that made you excellent can read to your team as "nothing is ever good enough." The decisiveness that got you promoted can read as "she doesn't listen." Watch especially for how your best qualities show up under pressure, because that is when strengths overshoot into derailers, and when your team is watching most closely.

✦ **AI ON YOUR TEAM**

Use an AI assistant as a sparring partner on your blind spots. Give it your top strengths and ask how each might overshoot into a derailer in a management role, and how you would recognize it early. Feed it the patterns from your personal audit and ask what they have in common. And have it pressure-test a decision you are about to make: where might my usual strength be leading me astray here? It cannot see you, but it is very good at naming the shadow you may be too close to notice.

THIS WEEK

1. List your top three or four strengths and, for each, the drawback it could become if overused here.
2. Run a quick personal audit: what has and has not gone well in your career, and what pattern connects the misses?
3. Name the one strength most likely to derail you in this role, and how you will catch it.
4. Add one or two deliberate adjustments to your action plan: strengths to lean on, behaviors to watch.

Tools: *Potential Drawbacks of Key Strengths, Common Derailers, Strengths and Derailers Checklist, and Personal Audit Sheet (in the Toolkit appendix, Chapter 9). Fillable versions are in the companion workbook and free at TheEmergentManager.com.*

PART II: IMMERSION (LEARN THE TERRAIN)

CHAPTER 10

Manage Up

Reading your boss, and flexing to fit

> ◎ **OUTCOME**
>
> By the end of this chapter you will be able to read your boss's working style along three dimensions and adapt to it without losing yourself, so the single most consequential relationship in your new role works for you rather than against you.

Of all the relationships you will manage in your new role, the one with your own boss is the most consequential, and the one new managers most often get wrong. Not because they are bad at it, but because they treat it as something that happens to them rather than something to be studied and shaped. Two managers report to the same director. One keeps getting blindsided, her updates ignored, her decisions second-guessed. The other learned in his second week that this director wants a three-line summary every Friday and no surprises, ever, and built his whole rhythm around it. Same boss, completely different experience. The difference was not luck. It was homework.

The research is blunt on this point: more than almost any other single factor, the quality of the relationship with your supervisor shapes whether you succeed, regardless of your level or your experience. The best of these relationships are built by real effort on both sides. But you cannot count on your boss to do their half, so your move is simple: do yours, starting with understanding how they actually work.

The three Ds

A useful way to read any power relationship, including the one with your boss, is along three dimensions. Distance is how much social distance your boss prefers: do they want a formal, role-to-role relationship, or a warmer, person-to-person one? Get this wrong, too familiar with a formal boss or too stiff with a warm one, and everything feels slightly off. Deference is how much they expect you to defer to their position, knowledge, and authority: some bosses want their call respected and expect to be consulted; others want you to push back and challenge them, and read silence as weakness. Divergence is how much deviation from their goals and methods they will tolerate: some want it done their way, others give you wide latitude as long as you hit the target.

Reading these three tells you how to operate. A boss who is high on deference and low on divergence wants to be consulted and wants it done their way; a boss who is low on deference and high on divergence wants you to challenge the plan and then run with your own. Neither is right or wrong. What is wrong is guessing.

Do your homework

Learn your boss's style the same way you learn anything about a person, through close observation and direct conversation, with your boss and with people who have worked with them. Pay attention to their communication style and, especially, their preferred mode: when do they want a face-to-face, and when would a two-line message do? Learn their most urgent priorities, the pressures and stresses they are under, and where they most need support from you.

Then, do the thing most people are too timid to do: ask. In your first weeks, sit down and have an explicit conversation about how they like to work. How often do they want updates, and in what form? What do they want to be looped in on, and what do they trust you to just handle? What does a great working relationship look like to them? Most bosses are pleasantly surprised to be asked, and almost none will volunteer the answers unprompted.

Flex without losing yourself

Once you understand the style, adapt to it. Flexing your style is not slavish conformity, and it is certainly not sucking up. It is translation. If your boss wants concise summaries, give them concise summaries, so your substance actually lands instead of getting lost in detail they will not read. Meeting your boss where they are on the things they care about, format, cadence, how much detail, buys you enormous latitude on the things you care about. Support them, too: understand what keeps them up at night and make that part of your world easier, and you become someone they come to rely on rather than someone they have to manage.

Then pass it on

Two follow-ups. First, actually change your habits to match what you learned; if your boss wants a Friday summary, the Friday summary has to appear on Fridays, or the whole exercise was theater. Second, remember that you are now a boss yourself, and your own direct reports are trying to read you exactly as you are reading your supervisor. Consider having the same kind of style conversation with them, telling them plainly how you like to work, which does for them what you wish every new boss had done for you.

The relationship with your boss is not weather you endure. It is something you build, deliberately, by reading their style and adapting to it on purpose. Get it right and your boss becomes your steadiest source of air cover, information, and opportunity. Get it wrong and even excellent work struggles to be seen. Few investments in your first months pay off faster.

⚠ WATCH OUT FOR

Two traps. The first is assuming your boss works the way you do, or the way your last boss did, and being repeatedly surprised when they don't. The second is mistaking managing up for flattery. Flexing your style is translation, not sycophancy, and it should never curdle into becoming the yes-person who never brings bad news. The best managed-up relationship includes honest pushback, delivered in the form your boss can actually hear.

AI ON YOUR TEAM

Use an AI assistant to decode and adapt. After a few interactions, describe your boss's behavior and ask it to characterize their likely style on distance, deference, and divergence, and how you might adjust. Have it help you plan the "how do you like to work" conversation. And when you have an update to send, ask it to reshape your messy draft into the exact format your boss prefers, whether that is a three-line summary or a one-page brief. It helps you translate; building the relationship is yours.

THIS WEEK

1. Read your boss on the three Ds: how much distance, deference, and divergence do they want?
2. Learn their communication preferences: what mode, how often, how much detail, and what they never want to be surprised by.
3. Have an explicit conversation in your first weeks: ask how they like to work and what a great relationship looks like to them.
4. Change one of your own habits to match, and consider having the same conversation with your direct reports.

Tool: *Supervisor Style Research Checklist (in the Toolkit appendix, Chapter 10). Fillable versions are in the companion workbook and free at TheEmergentManager.com.*

CHAPTER 11

Learn Faster

Diversify how you learn

> ◎ **OUTCOME**
>
> By the end of this chapter you will know the three ways people learn, which one you over-rely on, and how to widen your range so you get up to speed faster in a role where you have a great deal to learn.

In your first months there is more to learn than there is time to learn it: your boss and how they work, your team, your stakeholders, the technical guts of the job, the organization's politics and culture, the whole industry. Faced with that mountain, most of us reach for the one tool we always reach for. The natural reader buries herself in documents and never thinks to ask the person down the hall who already knows the answer. The natural doer dives in and figures it out by trial and error, skipping the memo that would have saved him a week. Both of them learn. Both learn slower than they could, because they are using one gear when the situation calls for all three.

There are, broadly, three ways to learn anything new. You can learn from people, by talking to those who know, asking, observing, being coached. You can learn from material, by reading, researching, and studying documents and data. And you can learn by doing, by experimenting and trying things and debriefing yourself afterward. Most of us lean heavily on one of these and neglect the other two, often without noticing. That is the trap. A one-dimensional learning style quietly limits both what you can learn and how fast you can learn it.

Know your default, then widen it

Start by being honest about which mode is yours. When something new lands on your desk, do you go find someone to talk to, go find something to read, or just start doing? There is no wrong answer, but there is a cost to using only one. So deliberately borrow from the strategies you under-use. If you are a reader, make yourself go ask three people this week what the documents will not tell you. If you are a talker, block the time to actually read the reports instead of relying on hallway summaries. If you are a doer, pause long enough to study before you leap. Widening your range feels awkward at first, because the new techniques are unpracticed, and that discomfort is exactly the sign you are stretching in the right direction.

Match the method to the material

Different things are learned best in different ways, and part of learning faster is choosing the right method for what is in front of you. The organization's culture and politics live in people's heads and hallway conversations, not in any document, so you learn them by talking and watching. The technical content of your role you might learn best from material and from doing. Your boss's style, as the last chapter showed, you learn by observation and a direct conversation. So when you hit something new, do not default. Ask a few quick questions instead: What exactly do I need to learn, and what matters most? What is the fastest way to learn it, and what are the alternatives? Who knows this best, and where is the most thorough source? What outside the organization, an industry report, a news article, would round out the picture?

Make it a habit

A new learning technique will not stick if you use it once and forget it. Pick one or two methods from your under-used strategies and build them into your routine, the same action plan you have been assembling since Chapter 1. Over a few months the payoff compounds quietly. A manager who can learn from people, from material, and from doing gets to competence faster on every front, and in a transition, where your central constraint is simply how much you do not yet know, speed of learning is one of the largest advantages you have.

The good news is that it is not a fixed trait. Your rate of learning is largely a function of how many ways you are willing to learn. Widen the range, match the method to the moment, and you will get up to speed on all of it, the people, the work, the place, faster than the manager beside you who only ever learns one way.

> ⚠ **WATCH OUT FOR**
>
> Your comfortable learning mode feels efficient because it is easy, not because it is fast. The reader who never asks misses the tacit knowledge that lives only in people's heads. The talker who never reads misses the detail. The doer who never studies repeats avoidable mistakes. When you notice yourself reaching for your usual mode on autopilot, treat that as the cue to deliberately try another one.

AI ON YOUR TEAM

AI is a powerful accelerant for two of the three modes: use it to research and summarize material quickly, and to rehearse things you want to learn by doing in a safe, low-stakes way. It can also generate the sharp questions you should be asking real people. The one thing it cannot do is replace the human conversations. The tacit knowledge about your boss, your team, and the culture lives in people, so let AI speed the reading and the practice, and spend the time it saves on the talking.

THIS WEEK

1. Name your default learning mode: people, material, or doing. Which do you over-rely on?
2. Take the learning inventory and pick two techniques from your under-used strategies to try this week.
3. For the biggest thing you need to learn right now, ask: what is the fastest way, and who knows it best?
4. Add one new learning technique to your action plan so it becomes a habit, not a one-off.

Tool: *Learning Techniques Inventory (in the Toolkit appendix, Chapter 11). Fillable versions are in the companion workbook and free at TheEmergentManager.com.*

CHAPTER 12

Read the Culture

The unwritten rules of how this place works

> ◎ **OUTCOME**
>
> By the end of this chapter you will know how to read an organization's culture and politics, the unwritten rules that decide what actually works here, so you can avoid the landmines and get things done the way this place gets things done.

Six weeks in, a capable new manager stood up in a staff meeting and proposed a change she was sure was right. It was right. It also died on the spot, and she could not understand why. What she did not know was that in this organization big ideas were always floated privately, one person at a time, and lined up before any meeting; raising something new in the open read as an ambush, a way of forcing people's hands. She had done nothing wrong by the rules of her last company. She had simply not yet learned the rules of this one. Every organization runs on an invisible operating system, and until you learn it, your best ideas can keep failing for reasons no one will say out loud.

Every organization has political and cultural systems, each with its own history, traditions, and rules of behavior, and most of those rules are unwritten. It is easy to step into a hole or trip a landmine completely by accident, especially if your Key Few Objectives require you to change things. So the astute move is to learn the culture on purpose and early, before you act, so you can predict how different people will react and judge which battles are actually worth fighting.

The right mindset is an anthropologist arriving in an unfamiliar society. You would not assume the customs of home apply here; you would observe, ask, and find local guides to interpret what you were seeing. Do the same. Your guides are your boss, your team, someone in HR, a coach, and a few trusted stakeholders. Use them to tell you how your messages and moves are likely to be heard before you make them, not after.

Learn the politics

Start with how power actually works here, which is rarely what the org chart shows. Ask how decisions really get made, and what gets people to yes: collaboration, negotiation, quiet persuasion? Find the real key players, formal and informal, and the influencers, the people who get things done regardless of their title. Learn whose support you need to move anything significant, and where the pockets of power sit. Is the place centralized or decentralized, and how much really lives at the corporate offices? The org chart gives you the formal structure. The politics give you the real one, and it is the real one you have to operate in.

Learn the culture

Then read the unwritten rules and the values underneath them. Do things move through the formal chain of command, or through informal networks? How does this place communicate, and what is genuinely the most effective way to be heard? Is the horizon short-term or long? How are performance problems handled, and how are differences of opinion dealt with, openly, offline, or not at all? Is risk-taking rewarded or quietly punished? What are the social traditions, the stories and legends people tell as touchstones? And underneath all of it, what does this organization actually value, creativity, loyalty, harmony, quality, efficiency? The answers tell you how to operate here without setting off alarms you did not know were wired.

Work with the grain, for now

Reading the culture is not the same as surrendering to it. The point is to move within it effectively while you build the standing to change the parts that need changing. Early on, work with the grain: get things done the way this place gets things done. That is what earns you the credibility to later push against the customs that hold your team back. Fighting the culture before you understand it just gets you labeled as someone who does not get it, and that label is expensive to shed.

So pick your battles deliberately. Predict how each constituency will react, weigh which fights are worth the political capital, and save your open resistance for the few that truly matter. You will spend your entire tenure inside this culture. The managers who thrive are the ones who learn to read it early, the anthropologists, rather than the ones who assume everyone everywhere plays by the rules of wherever they came from. Learn the unwritten rules, keep your local guides close, and you stop stepping on landmines and start moving things that other newcomers cannot.

⚠ **WATCH OUT FOR**

Two traps. The first is importing the rules of your last company; what worked brilliantly there can be exactly the wrong move here. The second is the confident newcomer who "tells it like it is" before earning the right to. Candor that ignores the local norms lands as arrogance, not courage. Read the culture to navigate it wisely, not to be absorbed by it, and not to announce your verdict on it in week three.

✦ **AI ON YOUR TEAM**

AI cannot feel a room, but it can help you prepare to read one. Use it to turn the politics and culture questions into a plan for who to ask what. After your conversations, feed it your notes and ask it to map the likely power players and the values the stories reveal. And before a significant move, have it play a skeptic from this specific culture: given how you have described the way this place works, how might this land, and with whom? The judgment stays yours; it just helps you rehearse.

THIS WEEK

1. Recruit two or three local guides (your boss, a savvy peer, someone in HR) to interpret the culture for you.
2. Work through the politics questions: how are decisions really made, and who are the true influencers?
3. Work through the culture questions: how does this place communicate, handle disagreement, and what does it truly value?
4. Before your next significant move, predict how each key group will react, and decide whether it is a battle worth fighting.

Tool: *Organizational Politics and Culture Research Checklist (in the Toolkit appendix, Chapter 12). Fillable versions are in the companion workbook and free at TheEmergentManager.com.*

PART II: IMMERSION (LEARN THE TERRAIN)

CHAPTER 13

Learn How Work Gets Done

The systems behind the work

> ◎ **OUTCOME**
>
> By the end of this chapter you will understand the organization's structure and the business processes that carry work into and out of your team, so you know whether the systems are helping your objectives or quietly working against them.

By month three, a new manager knew his people, had his boss figured out, and had learned to read the culture. And he was still getting blindsided, just from a different direction. A hire he needed sat for six weeks in an approval process he had not known existed. A budget request missed the capital-planning cycle by a week and had to wait a year. A project stalled because the unit upstream fed him what he needed late, every single time, and there was nothing personal about it; that was simply how their process ran. He had learned the people and the culture. He had not yet learned the plumbing.

Managers often stumble a few months in for exactly this reason: they never learned enough about the larger organization their team sits inside. What matters most here is the organization's business systems, its structure and the processes and procedures that actually move work. Once you understand how that machinery runs, you can see something you could not see before: whether the systems support your objectives or fight them, and where the flows that feed you, and the ones you feed, are helping or quietly holding you back.

Map the structure and the key processes

Start with the structure: how the organization is really put together, and where your team sits in the flow of work. Then learn the handful of processes and policies you will run into constantly. How does sales or service delivery actually work? How do new products get made? What are the financial cycles, the operating budget and the capital-budgeting calendar? What is the HR machinery, hiring, performance reviews, compensation, succession? How do purchasing and expenditures work, and what are the technology standards and security rules?

You do not need to master all of them. You need to know which ones your objectives depend on and how they truly run, timing very much included. A great deal of "why is this stuck?" turns out, on inspection, to be "you missed the cycle." Learn the calendars and the sign-off paths, and a whole category of nasty surprises simply stops happening to you.

See yourself as one unit in a system

Your team is not an island; it is a node in a larger system. It takes inputs from other units and hands outputs to others, and a surprising amount of your effectiveness is decided at those seams rather than inside your own group. So learn the handoffs. Which units feed you, and are their inputs timely and good? Which units depend on what you produce, and are you serving them well? When you can see the flow, you can partner with the units around you to fix the joints that are weak, which is often higher-leverage than anything you could do alone.

Do the systems help or fight your objectives?

Now the sharp question. Go back to your Key Few Objectives and ask honestly whether the organization's systems support them or work against them. Where a system is fighting you, you have three moves. You can work within it, by learning its rules and timing so you stop being ambushed. You can work around it, by finding the legitimate path that experienced people already use. Or you can work to change it, by partnering with stakeholders to improve the process itself. Early in your tenure, lean on the first two; changing a system is a later move that draws on credibility you are still building. While you are at it, look for leverage you are not using: what technology, training budget, or outside resources and affiliations are available that you could tap and currently are not?

The end of learning the terrain

With this, the immersion phase is complete. Over these last chapters you have come to know yourself, your strengths and their shadows, your boss, the culture, and now the machinery that carries the work. That was the whole purpose of this stretch: not to act yet, but to see clearly. The changes you make next will only ever be as good as your understanding of the place you are making them in, and you now understand it. You are no longer a stranger here. It is time to start reshaping.

⚠ **WATCH OUT FOR**

Two traps. The first is assuming the systems work the way they logically should. They rarely do; the real process lives in people's heads and quiet workarounds, not in the policy document. The second is trying to fix a broken system before you understand why it exists. Almost every awkward process was once someone's solution to a real problem. Learn the reason before you propose the change, or you may cheerfully recreate the very problem it was preventing.

✦ **AI ON YOUR TEAM**

Use an AI assistant to make sense of the machinery. Have it help you list the key processes your objectives depend on and the questions to ask about each. Feed it what you learn and ask it to flag where a process's timing or a handoff between units is likely to bite you. And when a system is fighting a goal, have it lay out the three options, work within it, around it, or to change it, with the trade-offs of each, so you choose deliberately rather than by default.

THIS WEEK

1. Sketch the organization's structure and where your team sits in the flow of work.
2. List the three or four business processes your Key Few Objectives most depend on, and learn how each actually runs, including its timing.
3. Map your team's key handoffs: which units feed you, which you feed, and where the seams are weak.
4. For each objective, ask whether the systems help or hinder, and decide whether to work within, around, or to change the ones that hinder.

Tool: *Business Systems Research Checklist (in the Toolkit appendix, Chapter 13). Fillable versions are in the companion workbook and free at TheEmergentManager.com.*

PART III: RESHAPING (MAKE YOUR MARK)

CHAPTER 14

Size Up Your Team

What your team has, and what it needs

> ◎ **OUTCOME**
>
> By the end of this chapter you will know how to assess your team's competencies against what your objectives actually require, find the gaps, and make a plan to close them, because your credibility rises and falls with the strength of your team.

Here is a truth that takes new managers a while to accept: your success is not really yours. It is your team's. A leader with a strong, well-matched team looks capable almost effortlessly, and the same leader with a weak or wrong-shaped team looks like they are failing no matter how many hours they put in. The credibility you spent your first months earning now rests largely on people other than you. Which makes the first act of reshaping a clear-eyed one: taking an honest measure of the team you inherited against the work you have been asked to do.

You have finished learning the terrain. Now you begin to change it, and the sensible place to start is not with grand plans but with the raw material you have to work with, your team. A competency is simply a knowledge base, skill, or ability a person or team needs to accomplish its objectives, things like strategic thinking, decision-making, customer focus, communication, developing others. Your question is not whether your team is good in some abstract sense. It is whether it has the specific competencies your Key Few Objectives require.

Do the gap analysis

The way to answer that is a systematic gap analysis, in four steps. First, assess the competencies needed to achieve your objectives. Start from the objectives, not from the people; ask what capabilities any team would need to deliver these results. Second, assess your team's current competencies, objectively, in evidence rather than in reputation. Third, analyze the gaps, the difference between what the work needs and what the team has. Be specific here: break each needed competency into observable component behaviors, and mark honestly which ones exist and which are missing. Fourth, build an action plan for closing the gaps you found.

The discipline in all of this is objectivity. You are assessing your team against the requirements of the work, not against how long people have been here, or how much you like them, or how things have always been done. That is harder than it sounds, because the people you are assessing are people you now know, but it is the only way the analysis tells you the truth.

Assessing people you rarely see takes longer and deserves more humility. You are working from a narrower sample, weighted toward whoever is most visible in writing and in meetings, which is not the same thing as whoever is most effective. Give the assessment more time, and gather more of your evidence from the people who work alongside them.

Closing the gaps

Once you can see the gaps clearly, you have a familiar set of levers, in rough order of first resort. You can develop the people you have, through training, coaching, and stretch assignments. You can redeploy, putting the right people on the right work so existing strengths land where they matter. You can hire, bringing in a capability the team simply does not have. And where a gap is persistent and development cannot close it in time, you can address underperformance directly. Most gaps close through development and redeployment; hiring and the harder moves come when the gap is large and the clock is short. Match the lever to the size of the gap and the time you have.

Be honest, and be fair

This is where clear eyes and a warm heart have to coexist. The assessment must be honest: pretending a gap is not there does not make it disappear; it just guarantees you miss your objectives, and your credibility with them. But the response should be fair. A gap is a development need, not a verdict on a person's worth, and most people can grow into what a role requires if you invest in them and are clear about what you need. The exception is the persistent gap that no reasonable development will close on the timeline you actually have, and those you will have to address directly, which is harder ground we will come to.

Sizing up your team is uncomfortable precisely because it is honest, and because the answer implicates you as much as them; a weak team is now your problem to solve. But it is the foundation of everything else in this phase. You cannot reshape what you have not measured. Do the gap analysis, and the moves that follow, who you develop, who you move, who you add, stop being guesses and become a plan.

⚠ **WATCH OUT FOR**

Two traps. The first is assessing people instead of capabilities; the goal is to map competencies against the work, not to grade personalities. The second is confusing "people I like" or "people who have been here longest" with "people who have what the objectives require." Loyalty and tenure are real and valuable, but they are not competencies. Assess honestly against the work, then act humanely toward the people.

✦ **AI ON YOUR TEAM**

Use an AI assistant to structure the analysis, not to make the judgments. Have it translate each Key Few Objective into the competencies and observable behaviors a team would need to deliver it. Feed it your honest read of the team and ask it to lay out the gaps and the range of ways to close each one, develop, redeploy, hire. Then take it back: judging real people is yours to do, with evidence and fairness. AI builds the frame; you make the calls.

THIS WEEK

1. List the competencies your Key Few Objectives actually require, starting from the objectives, not the people.
2. Assess your team's current competencies objectively, in evidence rather than reputation.
3. For each needed competency, break it into component behaviors and mark which exist and which are gaps.
4. Draft an action plan for the biggest gaps: develop, redeploy, hire, or address, matched to the gap and your timeline.

Tools: *Team Competency Gap Analysis Template and Sample (in the Toolkit appendix, Chapter 14). Fillable versions are in the companion workbook and free at TheEmergentManager.com.*

PART III: RESHAPING (MAKE YOUR MARK)

CHAPTER 15

Navigate Competing Agendas

Turning conflict into a workable deal

> ◎ **OUTCOME**
>
> By the end of this chapter you will be able to anticipate where your agenda will collide with other people's, and work through the conflict toward a resolution that gets you what you need without burning the relationship.

The moment you start trying to make a difference, you start bumping into other people's agendas. You launch an initiative that is obviously good for the company, and a peer digs in against it, not because your idea is bad, but because it quietly costs him something you never thought about: budget, headcount, control, a number he is measured on. This is not a sign that you are wrong. It is the ordinary physics of change. Any move worth making rearranges something for someone, and the people it rearranges will push back. The managers who make a real mark are not the ones who avoid conflict. They are the ones who see it coming and work through it well.

Conflict is simply built into interdependent workplaces: different goals, different priorities, different views of what should be done and how, and, often, competition for scarce resources. It gets sharper precisely when you are implementing change, which is your job now. And here is the part that is easy to forget: conflict can be healthy. Handled well, working through a clash of agendas is how you win stakeholder support, build synergies and strong relationships, and grow your credibility across the organization. Handled badly, or avoided, it does the reverse.

Anticipate it

Most conflict is predictable if you look for it. Before you roll anything out, put yourself in the shoes of everyone your initiative touches. Who is affected, and what do they stand to lose? Follow the consequences downstream, past the obvious first ripple. Has something like this been tried before, and how did people react? Which individuals or coalitions are most likely to resist, and in what form, open opposition, quiet foot-dragging, a competing proposal? Anticipating the conflict early lets you design around it, or prepare for it, instead of being ambushed by it in a meeting.

Clarify the agendas

When a conflict is real, bring it into the open and understand it honestly rather than guessing. What exactly is getting in the way of mutual support? What is your perspective and your genuine must-haves, and what are theirs? Then the question most people skip: what goals do you actually share? Almost every conflict contains more common ground than either side notices in the heat of it. And name the true basis of the disagreement, competition for resources, a real difference in philosophy, or a dispute about how the work should be done, because you resolve a resource fight very differently from a clash of values. Most conflicts feel personal and turn out, on inspection, to be structural.

Find a solution both can live with

The goal is not to win. It is to resolve the thing constructively, which usually means finding something both sides can support. Ask the generative question: if there were a solution that met both sets of needs, what would it look like? What does each of you actually need from the other? What are the alternative ways each of you could get that? And by what criteria will you decide? This is the difference between negotiating positions, I want this and you want that, and negotiating interests, what sits underneath each want. The workable deals almost always live at the level of interests, not positions.

Move forward, and follow through

A resolution is not real until it holds. Agree explicitly on how you will make sure it works for both of you, anticipate the barriers that could undo it and how you will clear them, and set up how you will support each other as you go. And when a conflict is genuinely thorny, you do not have to face it alone. Bring it to your advisory board, the small group of trusted advisors you assembled back in Chapter 1. A good advisor can help you see the other side's interests and pressure-test your approach before you are in the room, when it is still cheap to adjust.

The instinct of many new managers is to avoid conflict, to smooth things over and not make waves. But smoothing a conflict over does not resolve it; it just moves it underground, where it festers and resurfaces later, worse. The managers who reshape anything treat conflict as a normal, sometimes healthy, part of the work. They anticipate it, name it honestly, and negotiate their way to something both sides can stand behind. Do that, and each conflict you work through well leaves you with more support and more credibility than you had before, which is the exact opposite of what conflict usually costs.

⚠ **WATCH OUT FOR**

Two traps. The first is treating all conflict as bad; some of it is just the healthy friction of a good idea meeting reality, and avoiding it means avoiding progress. The second is treating conflict as a contest to win. Winning at someone's expense buys you a resentful loser and a weaker relationship, when what you needed was a resolution both could support. And watch for the most dangerous form of all: conflict avoidance disguised as harmony, where the disagreement goes unspoken and quietly undermines you.

✦ **AI ON YOUR TEAM**

Use an AI assistant to prepare for a hard conversation. Describe the initiative and the person likely to resist, and ask it to map what they might stand to lose and where your interests actually overlap. Have it help you separate positions from interests and brainstorm solutions that could satisfy both. Then have it play the other party so you can rehearse staying constructive under pressure. It cannot resolve the conflict for you, but it can make sure you walk in prepared rather than surprised.

THIS WEEK

1. Before your next initiative, list who it affects and what each stands to lose, following the consequences downstream.
2. For your sharpest current conflict, name your must-haves, the other side's, and the goals you share.
3. Identify the real basis of the conflict, resources, philosophy, or how to operate, and look for a solution that meets both sets of needs.
4. Bring a thorny challenge to a trusted advisor before you tackle it, and agree how you will make any resolution stick.

Tools: *Conflicting Agenda Checklist and Challenge Consultation Form (in the Toolkit appendix, Chapter 15). Fillable versions are in the companion workbook and free at TheEmergentManager.com.*

PART III: RESHAPING (MAKE YOUR MARK)

CHAPTER 16

Build an Inclusive Team

Where people feel safe to do their best work

> ◎ **OUTCOME**
>
> By the end of this chapter you will understand why psychological safety and inclusion are performance issues, not just values, and you will have concrete ways to build a team where difference is an asset and everyone can do their best work.

Picture a team with all the talent it needs that keeps falling short anyway. In its meetings, people hold back. Someone sees a risk and does not name it; the room defers to whoever speaks loudest; the quietest expert, the one holding the insight that would have changed everything, never says a word. The talent was never the problem. What the team lacks is the sense that it is safe to bring a real opinion into the room, and a culture inclusive enough that its newest and most different member will be heard when they do. That, more than talent, is one of the largest levers you have as a manager, and you are the one who builds it or breaks it.

The most reliable predictor of how well a team performs is not how smart its members are. It is psychological safety, a term the Harvard researcher Amy Edmondson coined for the shared sense that you can speak up, disagree, admit a mistake, or ask a naive question without being punished or made to feel small. On a psychologically safe team, problems surface while they are still small, ideas compete on merit rather than volume, and people take the smart risks that any real progress requires. Without it, the most important information a team has stays locked in people's heads. Google reached the same conclusion when it studied its own teams in a project it called Aristotle: of everything it measured, psychological safety mattered most.

Inclusion is the other side of the same coin. Diversity, defined broadly, not only ethnicity, gender, and age, but also learning style, background, education, and experience, gives a team more perspectives to draw on. But those perspectives only pay off when they are genuinely valued and heard, not merely present. A diverse team that is not inclusive gets all the friction of difference and none of the benefit.

This is a performance issue, not a poster

It helps to be clear that this is not only the right thing to do; it is the effective thing. Teams that are both diverse and inclusive generate better ideas and more innovation, because they have more angles to draw on. They make better decisions and learn faster. And they keep their best people, because employees who feel valued and treated fairly stay and give more. In a world where your customers, your talent pool, and your partners are all growing more diverse, a manager who works well across difference has a genuine and measurable edge.

Start with yourself

You cannot build an inclusive team while unaware of your own biases and blind spots, and everyone has them, the well-intentioned very much included. Bias rarely shows up as hostility. It shows up as a pattern of small defaults: whom you naturally listen to and whom you talk over, whose ideas you instinctively credit, who gets handed the visible, career-making assignments and who does not. The first move is simply to notice your own patterns, because you cannot correct a tilt you cannot see.

Build the safety, on purpose

Psychological safety is not created by announcing it. It is built in small, repeated behaviors. Invite dissent explicitly, ask "what am I missing?" and then genuinely thank the person who tells you. Admit your own mistakes and uncertainty out loud, which quietly gives everyone else permission to do the same. Make sure the quiet voices are heard and not just the loud ones, by calling on people, going around the room, or asking for input in writing. And above all, watch how you react the first time someone brings you bad news or disagrees with you, because that single moment teaches the whole team whether it is safe to do it again. Meet the first problem with curiosity instead of blame and the truth keeps coming; punish it once and the flow dries up for good.

Guard the edges, too. Notice who is quietly carrying too much and heading for burnout, who keeps getting left out of the conversations that matter, and who has gone silent lately. Inclusion is as much about who is at the table and how they are doing as it is about what gets said there.

Make it a habit, not an event

Finally, treat inclusion as an ongoing practice rather than a one-time training. Ask the honest questions. Does my team actually reflect a range of people and perspectives, or does nearly everyone look and think alike? Are people comfortable talking about difference, and how could I open that conversation in a healthy way? What is already working here that I can build on, and what current best practices could I bring in? A team where people feel safe and included is not a soft extra. It is, measurably, a higher-performing team, because it surfaces more truth, produces more ideas, and holds on to more of its best people. And of everything in the reshaping phase, this may be the part most within your direct control, because a team takes its cultural cues, more than from anything else, from the person leading it.

> ⚠ **WATCH OUT FOR**
>
> Two traps. The first is mistaking politeness for safety. A team where everyone is agreeable but no one ever disagrees is not safe, it is silent, and silence conceals the very problems you most need to hear. The second is treating inclusion as a checkbox or a poster on the wall rather than something you practice daily in how you run a meeting and hand out work. And remember: your reaction the first time someone brings you a mistake sets the tone for years.

> ✦ **AI ON YOUR TEAM**
>
> AI can hold up a mirror. From your meeting notes, ask it to flag who spoke and who did not, and whose ideas you built on, a simple check on your own patterns. Have it suggest ways to draw out quieter voices or to open a healthy conversation about difference. And use it to pressure-test a decision for the perspectives your team might be missing. But the safety itself is built by how you behave in the room, in the small moments no tool can handle for you.

THIS WEEK

1. Watch your own patterns for a week: who do you listen to, credit, talk over, and give the visible work to?
2. In your next meeting, explicitly invite dissent ("what am I missing?") and thank whoever offers it.
3. Make sure the quiet voices are heard, call on people or ask for input in writing, not just live.
4. Ask the inclusion questions: does my team reflect real difference, and are people comfortable talking about it?

Tool: *Inclusive Culture Checklist (in the Toolkit appendix, Chapter 16). Fillable versions are in the companion workbook and free at TheEmergentManager.com.*

PART III: RESHAPING (MAKE YOUR MARK)

CHAPTER 17

Craft a Vision Worth Following

A clear picture of where you are taking the team

> ◎ **OUTCOME**
>
> By the end of this chapter you will know how to craft a clear, motivating vision for your team, one grounded in real information and aligned with where the organization is going, so people know what they are working toward and why it matters.

A team can work extremely hard and still go nowhere in particular. People show up, clear their queues, hit their numbers, and yet if you asked any of them where the team is actually headed, you would get a shrug or five different answers. That is a team with effort but no direction, and it is a draining place to be, because nothing adds up to anything. A vision is what turns a group of busy people into a team pulling the same way. It is a clear picture of what you want your team to become, and it does something no amount of task management can: it tells people what they are working toward, and why it is worth the effort.

Whether you are making major changes or largely preserving how things run, you need a vision to focus your team and generate real commitment. A vision is a picture of what you want your unit to be, grounded in your read of where your industry and markets are heading, the challenges and opportunities ahead, and how your team can best meet them. Two things separate a real vision from a poster on the wall. It has to be grounded in actual information rather than wishful thinking, and it has to align with the organization's overarching vision, or your team ends up rowing hard against the direction of the whole company. A shared vision, one with genuine buy-in, begins with you designing the picture. Winning the team's commitment to it is the next chapter.

One honest note: because a vision is about the future, crafting one means facing uncertainty, which is uncomfortable. No one can be sure what is coming. But thinking systematically about what might come lets you point your team's energy in a promising direction, and that beats drifting every time.

Step one: gather information

Do not invent a vision alone at your desk. Gather first, and gather widely. Talk to a deliberately varied set of people: your team, your peers, and your boss, but also customers and suppliers, the people who usually disagree with you, fresh-eyed newcomers, seasoned strategists, and the occasional maverick who sees things sideways. Ask them about your unit's environment and its real role, its unique contribution, how it is perceived inside and outside the organization, who its key stakeholders are and what they need, and where your industry and markets are heading. Then go deep: make sure you understand the organization's overarching mission, vision, and values, because yours has to nest inside them.

Step two: analyze it

Turn all that information into an honest picture of your situation, essentially a clear-eyed assessment of strengths, weaknesses, opportunities, and threats. What are your team's real strengths, and how can you leverage them? Where can it make its greatest contribution, and what opportunities can it seize? Then the harder half:

what are its weaknesses, and how can you mitigate them? What threats need managing, and what do your customers quietly dislike that you could fix? A vision built only on aspiration is a fantasy. A vision built on an honest read of what is true is the beginning of a strategy.

Step three: design the vision

Now craft the picture. Given what you have gathered and analyzed, what should your team focus on, and what unique contribution should it make to the organization's mission? Who should its customers be, and what should it start doing, stop doing, and do better? What role should technology play, what culture do you need to build, and how should its performance be measured? And underneath all of it, the test question: what vision will actually energize the people you have and attract the people you want?

A good vision is specific enough to guide real decisions and vivid enough to move people. Vague uplift, "be the best," "delight our customers," guides nothing, because it rules nothing in and nothing out. Aim instead for a picture concrete enough that your team could look at a choice in front of them and ask, does this move us toward it, and actually answer.

Why it is worth the work

A vision is not a slogan you unveil once and forget. It is the north star that makes a thousand smaller decisions easier, because people can measure them against the picture themselves instead of routing everything through you. Crafting one well takes genuine effort, gathering, analyzing, designing, but that is the effort that turns you from a manager who keeps a team busy into a leader who is taking it somewhere. You have the picture now. The next chapter is about getting the team to make it theirs.

⚠ **WATCH OUT FOR**

Two traps. The first is writing the vision alone in a vacuum; a picture you invented at your desk, ungrounded and unshared, will be neither right nor believed. The second is confusing a vision with a slogan; a memorable phrase is not a vision, a vision is a picture specific enough to actually guide choices. And beware a vision, however inspiring, that ignores the organization's overarching direction, because it quietly sets your team against the company.

✦ **AI ON YOUR TEAM**

Use an AI assistant in the gathering and analysis steps, where it is strongest. Have it synthesize the input you collect into a clean strengths-weaknesses-opportunities-threats picture and surface patterns you might miss. Have it pressure-test a draft vision: is it specific enough to guide a decision, and does it align with the organization's stated mission? And ask it to sharpen vague language into a concrete picture. But the vision itself, the judgment about where this team should go, is yours. AI can organize the inputs and tighten the words; it cannot choose the direction.

THIS WEEK

1. Gather: talk to a deliberately varied set of people (team, customers, skeptics, newcomers, strategists) about where your unit and industry are heading.
2. Anchor: get clear on the organization's overarching mission and vision so yours can align to it.
3. Analyze: do an honest SWOT, strengths and opportunities to leverage, weaknesses and threats to manage.
4. Design: draft a one-paragraph picture of what your team should become, specific enough to guide a real decision.

Tools: *Vision Gathering, Analysis, and Design Checklists (in the Toolkit appendix, Chapter 17). Fillable versions are in the companion workbook and free at TheEmergentManager.com.*

PART III: RESHAPING (MAKE YOUR MARK)

CHAPTER 18

Win Commitment to the Vision

Turning your vision into the team's

> ◎ **OUTCOME**
>
> By the end of this chapter you will know how to turn the vision you drafted into one the team genuinely owns, by involving them in shaping it, building early wins, and working through resistance, so it captures both their minds and their hearts.

A manager once spent weeks crafting a genuinely good vision for his team. He wrote it up, polished the language, and unveiled it in a well-produced all-hands. People nodded. And then nothing changed. Six months later the vision was a slide no one referenced, because it had always been his, handed down, and nobody on the team felt it was theirs to carry. This is the trap that catches even the leaders who did the hard work of the last chapter: they mistake announcing a vision for sharing one. The power of a vision is not in the words. It is in whether the people who have to live it helped shape it, and chose to own it.

Drafting the vision was a real accomplishment, but it is only the first half of the job. The critical next step is to bring it to your team, involve them in refining and building on it, and win their genuine commitment, because a vision only does its work when it captures both minds and hearts. When it does, a shared vision gives people a sense of control over an uncertain future, focuses their effort, draws the team toward something worth reaching, bonds them around a common purpose, and converts the energy people usually tie up in anxiety about change into positive, task-focused energy. One caution: this is slow. Turning a personal vision into a truly shared one can take a year or more. It is still worth every bit of the effort.

Involve them in shaping it

The single biggest lever for ownership is co-creation. Bring the vision to your team not as a finished decree but as a strong draft to build on. Actively involve your key people, and the ones most affected, in refining it, and explicitly invite their reservations and concerns. You want the objections early, while you can still address them, rather than later as quiet resistance. And genuinely process what you hear; let the vision actually change based on their input. A vision people helped write is a vision people defend. A vision handed to them is one they merely tolerate.

Hold a visioning meeting

The best vehicle for this is not a circulated document but a meeting. A real visioning session engages you with the team and the team with the vision in a live, dynamic way, and the very act of investing time in it signals how much the vision, and their voice in it, matter. A few things make it work. Consider asking HR to facilitate, which frees you to listen and makes it easier for people to be candid. Go offsite to avoid interruptions. Have your direct reports lead parts of the agenda. Break into small groups so the feedback is honest. And end with each part of the team committing to what the vision means for them and what their next steps will be. Your job in that room is mostly to listen, not to sell.

Build early wins, and use your influencers

Commitment grows on evidence, not inspiration alone. So build in some early, visible wins that are strategically linked to the vision and that also help the broader organization, and celebrate them, so people can see the vision producing real results rather than just words. And put to use what you learned about the informal organization back in Chapter 12: identify the opinion leaders and influencers whose support moves other people, and bring them in early to help shape and champion the vision. A vision endorsed by the people others already trust travels far further than one pushed by the boss alone.

Work through the resistance

Some resistance to a vision is normal, and it usually comes from one of three places. It can come from negative past experience: people have watched a similar initiative fail before, and your job is to understand whether that failure was the idea, the execution, or the person behind it, and to speak to the real fear. It can come from a lack of control or input: people feel the change is being done to them, and the remedy is more genuine involvement, and sometimes simply slowing down, because you may be trying to do too much too soon. Or it can come from change itself feeling threatening: the loss of competence that comes with doing unfamiliar things, a clash with someone's personal values, or the plain anxiety of uncertainty, the sense that a known present beats an unknown future. Naming which kind of resistance you are facing tells you how to answer it, and turns a vague sense of pushback into something you can actually work with.

A vision becomes real not when you finish writing it but when your team stops calling it your vision and starts calling it our plan. That shift is slow, built through involvement, evidence, and patience, and it is the work that turns a picture in your head into a direction a whole team is pulling toward. With this, the reshaping phase is complete. You have sized up your team, worked through the conflicts, built a team where people can do their best work, and set and shared a vision that gives all of it direction. What remains is to make it stick.

> ⚠ **WATCH OUT FOR**
>
> Two traps. The first is presenting a finished vision and asking for buy-in you have no intention of acting on. People can smell fake consultation, and it breeds cynicism, not commitment; if you invite input, be genuinely willing to change something. The second is mistaking nodding and applause for commitment. Real commitment shows up in behavior over weeks and months, not in the room on the day. And do not rush it: a shared vision that takes a year is worth more than a slogan adopted in an afternoon.

> ✦ **AI ON YOUR TEAM**
>
> Use an AI assistant to prepare and to listen better. Have it help you design a visioning-meeting agenda that keeps you listening rather than presenting. Feed it the concerns your team raises and ask it to sort them into the three sources of resistance, past experience, lack of control, and fear of change, so you can address each on its own terms. And have it help you spot candidate early wins that advance the vision and help the wider organization. But the commitment itself is won in the room, by how genuinely you involve people, and no tool can do that part for you.

THIS WEEK

1. Bring the vision to your team as a strong draft to build on, not a finished decree, and invite their reservations openly.
2. Plan a visioning meeting (offsite, small groups, HR to facilitate if possible) where your job is mainly to listen.
3. Identify two or three early wins linked to the vision, and the opinion leaders who can help champion it.
4. For any resistance, name its source, past experience, lack of control, or fear of change, and address that specific fear.

Tools: *Vision Support-Building Checklist, Vision Resistance Checklist, and Vision Meeting Facilitation Guide (in the Toolkit appendix, Chapter 18). Fillable versions are in the companion workbook and free at TheEmergentManager.com.*

PART III: RESHAPING (MAKE YOUR MARK)

CHAPTER 19

Lead a Team You Rarely See

Building Trust, Rhythm, and Connection at a Distance

> ◎ **OUTCOME**
>
> By the end of this chapter you will understand why distance makes ordinary management harder rather than different, and you will have specific ways to build trust, run your team's rhythm, and coach well when you rarely share a room with the people you lead.

Elena took over a team of nine spread across three cities and two time zones. Two of them sat down the hall from her. The rest she saw only on a screen. She did what had always worked for her: she stayed available, she ran good meetings, she kept her door open. Four months in, her boss asked her why two of her strongest people kept getting passed over for the interesting work. Elena went looking for the answer and found it in her own calendar. Nearly every unscheduled conversation that quarter had been with the two people down the hall. She had never decided to favor them. She had simply been in the same building.

Nothing Elena did was wrong. What went wrong is that she kept relying on something that was no longer there. In a shared office a great deal of management happens for free. You overhear the context. You notice someone looks defeated on the walk to the coffee machine. Trust accumulates in a hundred small unplanned moments that nobody scheduled and nobody would think to put on an agenda. Take away the shared building and none of that stops mattering. It just stops happening by itself.

That is the idea worth carrying out of this chapter, and it is worth saying plainly: distance does not create new management problems, it removes the free solutions to the old ones. Everything you have built across this phase still holds and applies exactly as written. The difference is that proximity is no longer doing any of the work for you, so each of those things now has to be built on purpose.

The bias you will not notice

Start where Elena ended, because this is the failure mode almost every distributed manager walks into. The people you see get more of you. More of your attention, more of your informal coaching, more of the offhand context that turns out to matter, and, in time, more of the credit and the visible assignments. It is not a decision you make. It is a byproduct of who is physically in front of you, which is exactly what makes it so hard to catch. This is well documented. Researchers studying what they call passive face time, meaning the simple fact of being observed at work, found that people who are seen in the office get credited with being dependable and committed whether or not they have actually demonstrated either. A large field experiment at a Chinese travel company found that call center staff working from home were measurably more productive and far less likely to quit, yet were still promoted less often than their in-office peers performing at the same level. Careers stall for reasons nobody ever names, and the manager is usually the last to know.

The correction is not better intentions, it is measurement. Look honestly at your last month. Who did you talk to outside a scheduled meeting? Who got handed the interesting problem? Who have you not had a real conversation with since the spring? Write the names down in order. The pattern will be obvious, and once you can see it you can correct it, which is not true of a bias you are only vaguely worried about.

Design the rhythm, because it will not emerge

In an office, a team's rhythm partly assembles itself. At a distance you have to build it, and the pieces that used to be ambient are the ones you have to make explicit. Your one-on-ones stop being a good practice and become the primary channel, which means the rule is that you do not cancel them, least of all with the people you see least, because for them it is the only guaranteed access to you. Separate the meeting where you share context from the meeting where you track status, because when the two are merged the context is always what gets cut for time, and context is the thing distance destroys first.

Then write things down. Default to writing for decisions, reasoning, and anything that changed, not because writing is pleasant but because a distributed team runs on a written record and the alternative is a team where only the people in the right meeting know why. And watch how the schedule distributes its pain. If the recurring meeting always lands at six in the morning for the same person, that is not a neutral calendar, it is a quiet message about whose time counts, and everyone on the call can read it.

Trust at a distance is mostly reliability

In person, warmth carries a great deal of the load. You are around, you are decent to people, and it accrues. On a screen you have far less warmth available and far fewer moments to spend it in, and what fills the gap is predictability. Do what you said you would do, by when you said you would do it. Answer. Close the loop. Say so plainly when you cannot. Small reliability, repeated, is what people at a distance read as trustworthy, largely because it is most of what they can actually see of you.

Be deliberately human anyway. Distance strips out the accidental disclosure, the family photo on the desk, the reason you looked tired on Tuesday, and without it people fill the silence with their own guesses, which are rarely generous. A small amount of intentional openness travels further over a screen than it ever needed to in an office.

Coach through a screen

This is the hardest part, because video flattens signal. You lose the pause, the shift in posture, the thing that finally gets said in the hallway on the way back to the desk. So compensate on purpose. Ask more directly than you would in person. Ask the second question, the one after the answer that sounded fine. Leave the silence long enough to be slightly uncomfortable, because on a call most people will fill it and what they fill it with is usually the real answer. Check understanding out loud rather than assuming the nod meant yes.

And hold the hard conversations on a call with cameras on, never in a chat window and never over email. Written words carry no tone, so the reader supplies their own, and a person receiving difficult feedback almost always supplies the worst available reading. The inconvenience of finding thirty minutes is far cheaper than the month you will spend repairing a message that landed wrong.

Make the hybrid meeting fair

Hybrid is harder than fully remote, and managers consistently underestimate this. When part of the group is together in a room and the rest are on a screen, the screen loses every time. The side conversation, the whiteboard, the shared glance, the shorthand that develops among people who eat lunch together, none of it reaches the people dialing in, and they end up participating in a meeting they can only partly perceive. The simplest fix is also the fairest one: if anyone is remote, everyone is remote, one person to one screen. It costs the people in the building a little convenience and it buys the people outside it a genuine seat.

None of this is exotic, and that is rather the point. You are not learning a separate discipline called remote management. You are taking the things this phase has already asked of you, seeing your team clearly, building a culture where people speak up, setting a direction and winning real commitment to it, and doing them without the building that used to help. The managers who struggle at a distance are usually not the ones who lack some special skill. They are the ones who never noticed how much the building was doing, and so never replaced it.

> ⚠ **WATCH OUT FOR**
>
> Three traps. The first is confusing activity with contribution, watching green dots, response times, and hours logged. It tells you almost nothing about the work and it tells your team loudly that you do not trust them, which costs you far more than whatever you thought you were learning. The second is over-correcting with meetings, since adding a daily check-in feels like leadership but usually just taxes the people furthest from your time zone. The third, and the one that catches good managers, is assuming your own preference is neutral. If you like being in the office, you will reward the people who come in without ever deciding to.

AI ON YOUR TEAM

Distance runs on written context, which is exactly the work most managers skip because it takes time they do not have. This is where AI earns its place. Turn a meeting recording into a decision log so the people who could not attend are not a week behind by Monday. Draft the weekly context note, then edit it into your own voice. Have it summarize what changed and why, for the people who were not in the room. You can even ask it to look across your calendar and tell you who you have spent the least unscheduled time with this month, which is Elena's problem caught early. What it cannot do is any of the trust. That still comes down to whether you show up when you said you would.

THIS WEEK

1. Audit last month's calendar: who did you speak with outside a scheduled meeting, and who did you not? Write the names in order, most contact to least.
2. Protect the one-on-ones with the people you see least, and commit to never canceling them.
3. Pick one recurring hybrid meeting and run it one person, one screen.
4. Write down one decision you would normally have just said out loud, including the reasoning behind it, and put it where the whole team can find it.

Tool: *Distributed Team Working Agreement, with a completed example (in the Toolkit appendix, Chapter 19). Fillable versions are in the companion workbook and free at TheEmergentManager.com.*

PART IV: CONSOLIDATION (MAKE IT STICK)

CHAPTER 20

Deepen the Relationships That Carry You

Keeping the relationships you built strong

> ◎ **OUTCOME**
>
> By the end of this chapter you will know how to keep your key relationships healthy over time, deepening the strong ones, repairing the strained ones, and maintaining all of them, so the support you built early is still there when you need it most.

Back in your first months, you mapped your stakeholders and did the work of building relationships with the ones who mattered. Then you got busy, sizing up the team, setting a vision, driving change, and the relationships slipped down the list. Six months later a manager in exactly this position looks up and finds that a key ally, the one who used to champion his projects, has gone quiet and slightly cool. Nothing dramatic happened. He simply stopped tending the relationship, and relationships that are not tended do not hold steady; they decay. In the consolidation phase, keeping the relationships you built alive is not a nice-to-have. It is how you make sure the support you earned early is still there when the hard moments come.

Relationships are dynamic, and so are the forces that strain them. Every leader has to monitor the health of their stakeholder relationships, and for a new manager driving ambitious change, that monitoring matters even more, because change itself strains relationships, and you need them at full strength precisely when you are asking the most of people. So take stock, regularly, of where each key relationship actually stands, and then act on what you find. This is a good place to involve your team, too; they deal with these stakeholders as well, and they often see strains you have missed.

Take the temperature

Start with an honest assessment of each key relationship. A simple gauge works well: on a scale of one to ten, how strong was this relationship when you started, and where is it now? That before-and-after tells you which relationships have grown, which have held steady, and which have quietly slipped. Look for the strains you did not see coming, and for the style differences between you and a stakeholder that create friction when they go unaddressed. And ask the blunt question about each one: does this relationship need repair? Naming the answer honestly is the whole point of the exercise.

Deepen the strong ones

For the relationships that are working, do not simply coast on them; deepen them. Ask how strengthening this relationship could make both of your units more effective, where you could improve the efficiencies between you, and what barriers you could remove by working together. Ask what you could learn from each other and how you could put each other's talents to better use. The best working relationships are not merely cordial; they create synergy, each side quietly making the other better. That is worth actively building, not just preserving, and the strong relationships you invest in now are the ones that will carry your changes when it counts.

Repair the damaged ones

When a relationship is strained or broken, diagnose before you try to fix. How was it damaged, what is the history, and who was involved? What is really at the core, a lack of trust, conflicting agendas, a credibility problem? And what is the damage costing the business, in lost productivity, missed synergies, or lower quality? Then repair deliberately. The most powerful first move is usually to take honest ownership of your own unit's contribution to the problem, which almost always exists, and which disarms the other side more than any argument could. From there, open the communication to understand each other's perspective, bring in HR or an outside mediator if you are truly at an impasse, and agree on how you will communicate better going forward. Repair is slower and harder than maintenance, which is exactly why you do not want to let good relationships decay into needing it.

Make it a habit

None of this is a one-time audit. Relationships need ongoing attention, so build the stock-taking into your rhythm and add specific enhancement or repair actions to the same action plan you have carried since Chapter 1. The relationships you built in your first months are an asset that either compounds or erodes, depending entirely on whether you tend it. In the consolidation phase, when you are working to make your changes permanent, those relationships are the difference between changes that stick because people support them and changes that quietly unwind because the support beneath them was allowed to fade. Keep them strong, and they will carry you.

⚠ **WATCH OUT FOR**

Two traps. The first is treating relationship-building as a task you finished in month two; relationships you stop tending decay, and the decay is invisible until it is suddenly not. The second is waiting until a relationship is broken to pay it any attention, when repair costs far more than maintenance and some damage never fully heals. And when you do repair, resist the urge to lay all the blame on the other side; owning your part is almost always the fastest way through.

✦ **AI ON YOUR TEAM**

Use an AI assistant to keep the map current and to prepare for the hard conversations. Have it help you build a simple health tracker for your key relationships and prompt you when one has gone quiet. When a relationship is strained, describe the history and ask it to help you diagnose the core issue and separate your contribution from theirs. And have it help you plan a repair conversation that leads with ownership. But the relationship itself is rebuilt in person, by showing up and following through, which no tool can do for you.

THIS WEEK

1. Rate each key relationship one to ten, where it was when you started and where it is now, and flag the ones that slipped.
2. For a strong relationship, pick one way to deepen it, an efficiency to improve or a barrier to remove together.
3. For a strained one, diagnose the core issue, take honest ownership of your part, and plan a repair conversation.
4. Add specific relationship actions to your action plan, and ask your team where they see strains you might have missed.

Tools: *Relationship Maintenance and Enhancement Checklists (in the Toolkit appendix, Chapter 20). Fillable versions are in the companion workbook and free at TheEmergentManager.com.*

PART IV: CONSOLIDATION (MAKE IT STICK)

CHAPTER 21

Lock In Support for the Long Haul

The broad base a change needs to last

> ◎ **OUTCOME**
>
> By the end of this chapter you will know how to build the wide, cross-organizational support your vision needs to survive, by making the case in terms people actually care about, anticipating resistance, and closing the gaps that would otherwise erode it.

Your team is all in. You did the work of the last two chapters, crafted a vision and won their commitment, and the energy inside your unit is real. And then the initiative stalls anyway. Not because anyone openly killed it, but because a peer in another department never got behind it, a finance gatekeeper kept it low on the priority list, and a skeptical vice president two levels up quietly withheld the nod it needed. None of them fought you. They simply did not help, and their non-support was enough. This is the hard lesson of the consolidation phase: commitment inside your own team is necessary, but it is nowhere near sufficient. A change that lasts needs a critical mass of support well beyond your own walls.

Implementing a vision depends on the buy-in and effort of many people, departments, and constituencies beyond your immediate function. However good you are at creating a vision and winning your own team's commitment, you will also need supporters across the organization: key decision-makers, powerful peers competing for the same resources, and the stakeholders who actually carry out the work. And here is the sobering part, worth knowing before you learn it the hard way: even strong support from the very top is often not enough on its own. Changes die in the middle of an organization all the time, no matter who blessed them at the top, when the broad base of support underneath simply is not there.

Make the WIIFM clear

The core of winning support is easy to state and hard to do: every stakeholder has to see, and believe, the WIIFM, the answer to "what's in it for me?" People support what serves their interests, not what serves yours, and there is nothing cynical about that; it is simply how organizations work. So for each key stakeholder, translate your vision into their terms. What does it give them, solve for them, or protect for them? This is far easier if you involved them in designing the vision back in Chapter 18, because they have already found their own stake in it. Where you did not, do the translation work explicitly, and honestly, do not manufacture a benefit that is not really there, because people can tell, and it costs you the trust you are trying to build.

Anticipate reactions at every juncture

Support is not won once and banked. It is won again and again as the rollout unfolds. So at each critical juncture, pause and ask what each key stakeholder's reaction to your next move is likely to be, and where resistance might surface. Anticipating reactions in advance lets you address concerns before they harden into opposition, the same proactive stance you took toward conflict in Chapter 15. The vision support-building and vision resistance tools you already have are built for exactly this; use them to plan each stage deliberately rather than reacting to surprises after the fact.

Close the gaps that erode support

Support also drains away when a vision keeps hitting walls, so part of locking it in is removing the organizational gaps that make the vision hard to execute. There are usually a handful. Skill and knowledge gaps on the team, which you close through development or hiring. Motivation gaps, where the leadership approach, the expectations, or the incentives are not actually pulling people toward the vision. Resource gaps. Policy and process gaps, where the rules for compensation, succession, or how resources get allocated are quietly working against your objectives rather than for them. And a values gap, closed only when you visibly model the new values yourself. Every one of these, left open, is a place where support leaks away, because people lose faith in a vision that never quite becomes real. Closing them keeps the vision credible, and the support behind it intact.

Follow through, and use your board

Building support is ongoing work: keep communicating the vision, keep delivering the visible wins, and keep checking where support is thinning. And lean on your personal advisory board from Chapter 1 here, because a trusted advisor can often tell you where you are quietly losing people that you cannot see from the inside. A vision with deep support inside your team and thin support outside it will stall the first time it needs something from someone who does not care about it. Building the broad base, patiently, stakeholder by stakeholder, in terms each of them values, is what turns a change you are pushing into a change the organization is carrying. That, in the end, is what "make it stick" really means: enough people, in enough places, actually want it to succeed.

⚠ WATCH OUT FOR

Two traps. The first is assuming top-down authority is enough; changes die in the middle of organizations regardless of who approved them at the top. The second is pitching your vision in your own terms rather than theirs; people do not adopt your priorities out of goodwill, they adopt what serves them. And remember that silent non-support is as fatal as open resistance and far harder to spot, so look for who is not helping, not only for who is objecting.

AI ON YOUR TEAM

Use an AI assistant to map and translate. For each key stakeholder, have it help you articulate the specific WIIFM, what your vision actually does for them. Have it anticipate the reactions and objections at each stage of the rollout so you can pre-empt them. And feed it your list of execution gaps and ask it to rank which ones, left open, would most undermine support. But the support itself is earned in the conversations you still have to have, one stakeholder at a time.

THIS WEEK

1. List the stakeholders beyond your team whose support (or non-resistance) your vision needs, and rate where each stands.
2. For each, write the honest WIIFM, what your vision does for them, in their terms.
3. Anticipate reactions at your next rollout juncture, and address the likely concerns before they harden.
4. Identify the biggest gap (skill, resource, policy, values) that is eroding support, and a plan to close it.

Tools: *Closing the Gaps Strategy Checklist (Chapter 21); the Vision Support-Building and Vision Resistance Checklists (Chapter 18) also apply. Fillable versions are in the companion workbook and free at TheEmergentManager.com.*

PART IV: CONSOLIDATION (MAKE IT STICK)

CHAPTER 22

Measure Progress and Plan What's Next

Taking stock, and the road ahead

> ◎ **OUTCOME**
>
> By the end of this chapter you will know how to take an honest measure of your first six months, adjust your priorities for what comes next, and set yourself up to keep growing, because a transition does not really end. It becomes the way you lead.

Somewhere around the six-month mark, the frantic newness fades. You stop bracing every morning, you know the names and the systems and the unwritten rules, and one day you realize you are not the new manager anymore. Most people never mark this moment; they just keep going. But pausing here, to take honest stock of what you have achieved, what you have learned, and what still needs work, is one of the highest-leverage hours you will spend all year. It is the difference between drifting into your second six months and steering into them.

The whole point of a deliberate transition was to accelerate your success in the role, and a crucial final move is to evaluate how it went. A good evaluation does three things: it gauges how far you have actually come, it shows you where you need to fine-tune, and it tells you whether your Key Few Objectives themselves need updating, because the world and the role have both moved since you set them. And it is not a solo exercise. Do it with your boss, and consider pulling in HR for another perspective; the same people who helped you set your direction are the ones who can best help you judge it.

Take honest stock

Measure yourself against the things you actually set out to do. How much progress have you made on each Key Few Objective? Where do your Role Charter or your objectives now need updating? How well did you execute the action plan you have carried since Chapter 1? What are your most important strengths at this point, and where do you most need to keep developing? An honest self-assessment, checked against how your boss and others actually see it, that self-versus-others gap from Chapter 8, one more time, tells you where you truly stand rather than where you hope you stand.

Adjust, don't just record

The value of taking stock is entirely in what you change because of it. If a Key Few Objective is no longer the right one, update it; the discipline of focus from Chapter 2 matters just as much now as it did on day one. If a part of the role has been quietly neglected, redirect your attention there. An evaluation that does not change what you do next quarter was only paperwork.

Plan continued success

A transition does not so much end as graduate into ordinary leadership. So set a roadmap for what comes next: the objectives for your next phase, the skills you will keep building, the relationships you will keep tending, and the personal advisory board from Chapter 1 that you will keep consulting. Here is the quiet truth of the whole book: the habits that carried you through the transition, clarity about priorities, honest self-awareness, tending relationships, learning in every direction, are not transition habits. They are leadership habits, and the managers who keep them are the ones who keep rising.

The whole arc, in one look

Look back at the ground you have covered. You took hold: you prepared your entry, found the few things that mattered, started well with your team, mapped the people who matter, met resistance with a level head, and earned early credibility. You immersed yourself: you learned how change works, came to know yourself, played to your strengths, read your boss, learned faster, read the culture, and learned how work really gets done. You reshaped: you sized up your team, navigated competing agendas, built a team where people could do their best work, and crafted a vision and won the team's commitment to it. And you consolidated: you deepened the relationships that carry you, locked in broad support, and, here at the end, measured your progress and planned what is next. That is a complete transition, run on purpose instead of left to luck.

A last word

None of this was about being a natural. It was about having a plan and working it, one deliberate move at a time. You were handed a team and a title and, like almost every new manager, very little else. Everything you built from there, a team that trusts you, a direction worth following, the standing to lead, you built on purpose, in a hundred small, deliberate acts. So keep the habits. Keep the plan. And when the next new manager turns up looking lost in their first week, remember that you once did too, and hand them what you wish someone had handed you.

On Friday you were one of the best people on your team. On Monday you were responsible for it. Now, months on, you are something else again: a manager who knows what they are doing, and who got there not by luck, but by design.

⚠ WATCH OUT FOR

Two traps at the finish line. The first is declaring victory and stopping; the transition ends, but the leading does not, and the manager who coasts after six months is the one who plateaus. The second is taking stock without honesty; an evaluation you grade generously teaches you nothing, because the value is entirely in the parts that are hard to admit. Bring the same clear eyes to your own progress that you learned to bring to your team's.

AI ON YOUR TEAM

Use an AI assistant to structure your review and your roadmap. Have it turn the progress-evaluation questions into a self-assessment you can complete, then help you compare your read with your boss's feedback and flag the gaps. And ask it to draft a roadmap for your next two quarters, objectives, skills, and relationships, starting from where you are now. But the honest reckoning, and the resolve to act on it, are yours alone.

THIS WEEK

1. Do an honest progress review: how far have you come on each Key Few Objective, and how well did you execute your action plan?
2. Update what needs updating, your Role Charter, your Key Few Objectives, the parts of the role you have neglected.
3. Sit down with your boss (and perhaps HR) to compare your read of your progress with theirs.
4. Draft a roadmap for your next two quarters, and keep consulting your advisory board.

Tools: *The Progress Evaluation (the same questions answered from three perspectives, self, supervisor, and HR) and the Roadmap for Continued Success (in the Toolkit appendix, Chapter 22). Fillable versions are in the companion workbook and free at TheEmergent-Manager.com.*

APPENDIX

The Emergent Manager Toolkit

Every tool from the book, organized by chapter, ready to use with a pen.

Each chapter's *This Week* box points to its section here. Everything below is fully usable in print. If you would rather fill the tools in on a screen, or want the complete, connected set for all twenty-two chapters in one place, that is the companion workbook; a free starter kit lives at TheEmergentManager.com.

Chapter 1: Prepare for Your Role

Four tools for shaping your entrance and lining up support: a plan for how you are announced, a sample announcement to adapt, a worksheet for your advisory board, and an action plan to track it all.

1.1 Appointment Communication Plan

Think through these questions and discuss your preferences with your boss and HR before any announcement goes out.

Appointment Communication Plan
Note your preferences, then confirm them with your supervisor.

a. When will the announcement be made?

b. To what audience (entire organization, department, key outsiders, partners)?

c. Through what channels (memo, newsletter, email, group chat, a few words from your boss, a short video)?

d. Any special situations to handle with care (a passed-over candidate, your predecessor)?

e. What are the most important messages you want the announcement to land?

IF IT ALREADY WENT OUT

If communications about your role were distributed without your input, get copies, learn how they landed in different quarters, and talk through any sensitive issues with your boss and HR.

1.2 Sample Appointment Memo

A model to adapt, not copy. Notice how it honors the outgoing manager, signals modest change rather than upheaval, and promises to listen first.

To: Customer Support Team
From: David Osei, Director, Customer Experience
Date: March 3
Re: Maya Rivera named Manager, Customer Support (Tier 2)

I'm pleased to announce that Maya Rivera will step into the role of Manager, Customer Support (Tier 2), effective March 10, reporting to me. Maya takes over from Chris Bell, who is moving on to lead our Product Support group. Chris grew this team from four people to twelve and set a standard of care we fully intend to build on, and has kindly agreed to help with a smooth handoff over the next few weeks.

Many of you already know Maya. She has spent three years on this team as a senior specialist, and she is often the person who quietly untangles our hardest tickets. In her new role she will focus on the priorities we have talked about as a group: faster first responses, a knowledge base that helps customers help themselves, and a team people want to stay on.

Maya's first few weeks will be about listening. She plans to meet with each of you before proposing any changes. Please give her the same candor and support you have given me, and join me in congratulating her.

1.3 Personal Advisory Board Worksheet

Name the perspectives you will need, then a person who can offer each. Aim for a small group you can actually call on.

My position

My Key Few Objectives for the first year

Perspective you want on your board	Possible advisory board member(s)
1. Knows this position well	
2. Understands my responsibilities	
3. Can help me map strategy on key issues	
4. Shows sound judgment	
5. Reads the politics; easy to talk with	
6. Genuinely cares about my success	
7. Has a track record with objectives like mine	
8. Other:	

1.4 Action Plan

Your master tracker. As you move through the book, capture the specific actions you commit to, with a due date, so intentions become commitments.

Chapter	Your action item(s)	Due	Done
Part I: Taking Hold			
1. Set the Stage Before You Start			
2. Find the Few Things That Matter			
3. Start on the Right Foot			
4. Map the People Who Matter			
5. See Resistance Coming			

Chapter	Your action item(s)	Due	Done
6. Earn Credibility Fast			
Part II: Immersion			
7. Understand How Change Works			
8. Know Yourself			
9. Play to Your Strengths			
10. Manage Up			
11. Learn Faster			
12. Read the Culture			
13. Learn How Work Gets Done			
Part III: Reshaping			
14. Size Up Your Team			
15. Navigate Competing Agendas			
16. Build an Inclusive Team			
17. Craft a Vision Worth Following			
18. Win Commitment to the Vision			
19. Lead a Team You Rarely See			
Part IV: Consolidation			
20. Deepen the Relationships That Carry You			
21. Lock In Support for the Long Haul			
22. Measure Progress and Plan What's Next			

Chapter 2: Find the Few Things That Matter

Three tools for naming your Key Few Objectives and locking them in: the Role Charter template, a research checklist to prepare it, and a completed example.

2.1 Role Charter Template

Draft this from your current understanding, then use it to guide the confirmation conversation with your boss. Aim to keep it to a single page once complete.

HEADER

Date finalized; your name and title; who you report to; any dotted-line relationships; who should confirm this charter.

I. Role Focus

IA. Scope of Responsibilities

Summarize your key responsibilities from the position description.

IB. Key Few Objectives

The 2 to 4 must-achieve accomplishments that will be the chief measure of your success; include any deadlines.

IC. Decision-Making Authority

Your authority for budget, hiring, termination, contracts, and other key decisions.

II. Relationship Focus

IIA. Supporting Your Supervisor's Objectives

How your boss would like you to support their own objectives.

IIB. Other Key Relationships to Manage

Names and positions of key people above, below, and lateral to you.

IIC. Preliminary Feedback Plan

Communication channels and frequency with your boss, plus other early feedback sources.

III. Development Focus

IIIA. Key People Resources

Mentors, backers, and a personal advisory board, and the support each offers.

IIIB. Other Development Opportunities
Development activities agreed upon, and their timing.

IV. Other Commitments

IV. Other Commitments
Any other commitments, agreements, and expectations related to your role.

Chapter 2: Find the Few Things That Matter, continued

2.2 Role Charter Research Checklist

Work through these before you finalize your charter. You will not have every answer on day one; the point is to know which questions to ask, and of whom.

1. Pinpointing the Key Few Objectives

- ☐ **KFOs:** What are the two or three must-achieves of the position?
- ☐ **Relative urgency:** What are the timeframes for each?
- ☐ **Success metrics:** What will success look like, and how will it be measured?
- ☐ **Staying current:** How will you check in with your boss to confirm these remain the key few?

2. Understanding the KFOs in Context

- ☐ **Alignment:** How do your KFOs contribute to the organization's results?
- ☐ **Key stakeholders:** Who are they, and do they (especially your boss's boss) agree on these priorities?
- ☐ **Managing dissent:** If stakeholders disagree, how can that be resolved?
- ☐ **History:** What has been tried before, and how did the organization react?
- ☐ **Obstacles:** What are the likely barriers, and how will you work around them?
- ☐ **Resistance:** Was there an internal candidate for your role? What is their likely reaction?

3. Resource Inventory and Authority

- ☐ **Staffing and resources:** Does your team have the skills and budget to achieve the KFOs? What is missing?
- ☐ **Information:** What are your need-to-knows before moving?

- [ ] **Authority:** Do you have the authority (hiring, spend, contracts) to deliver? If conditional, what are the conditions?

Chapter 2: Find the Few Things That Matter, continued

2.3 A Completed Example

A finished Role Charter for a first-time manager, Maya Rivera, newly promoted to lead a customer support team. Use it to gauge the level of specificity to aim for, especially in the Key Few Objectives.

Header

- Date finalized: March 3. Manager: Maya Rivera, Manager, Customer Support (Tier 2).
- Reports to: David Osei, Director, Customer Experience. Dotted-line: Priya Nair, Product Manager (escalations).
- Confirm with: David Osei (supervisor); Sam Cole (HR).

IB. Key Few Objectives

- By end of Q2: launch a self-service knowledge base for the top 20 issues, deflecting 15 percent of tickets.
- By end of Q3: cut average first-response time from 9 hours to under 4.
- By end of Q4: reduce voluntary team turnover from 25 percent to under 12 percent.

IC. Decision-Making Authority

- Set team schedules, priorities, and workflows.
- Hire for the one open role; terminations recommended jointly with David and HR.
- Approve team expenses under 500 dollars.

IIB. Other Key Relationships

- Priya Nair, Product (escalations); Julian Lee, Engineering (bug triage); Sam Cole, HR; Dana Wolfe, senior agent and passed-over internal candidate.

III. Development

- Advisory board: David Osei (sponsor), Priya Nair (cross-functional influence), Rosa Alvarez (peer manager, first-time-management mentor).
- Complete the Emergent Manager program in the first six months.

Chapter 3: Start on the Right Foot

Two tools for your first weeks with the team: a guide for your early meetings, and the questions behind a manager assimilation session.

3.1 Meeting Navigation Guide

Your first team meeting
Aim to do these, in the room.

- ☐ Be positive, confident, and direct.
- ☐ Honor the past and the team's contributions; speak to their strengths.
- ☐ Describe your background briefly, and be humble.
- ☐ Say you plan to build on the team's strengths.
- ☐ Tell them you will spend your first weeks learning, with one-on-ones to come.
- ☐ Emphasize teamwork; speak in "we," not "I."
- ☐ Say you will rely on them as they rely on you, and make no promises you cannot keep.
- ☐ Invite questions, and do a lot of listening.

Your one-on-ones
Ask and listen first; only then share, briefly, how you like to work.

Ask each person about:

- ☐ **The individual:** background, career, and proudest accomplishments.
- ☐ **Their function:** what role it plays, its wins and challenges, ideas for improvement.
- ☐ **The business:** the major challenges and opportunities they see.
- ☐ **The culture:** who succeeds here, how people communicate, how decisions get made.
- ☐ **The team:** its biggest strengths, challenges, and ways to contribute more.

- ☐ **Advice for you:** on key stakeholders, and anything you have not thought to ask.

> **A CAUTION**
> In these first meetings, steer away from discussions of career goals or advancement. Those conversations matter, but they belong to a later date.

3.2 Manager Assimilation Meeting Guide

The questions a facilitator commonly asks your team, meeting without you, in an assimilation session. Their anonymous answers become the agenda for your conversation with the team.

- ☐ **1.** What do you already know about the new manager? What do you still have questions about?
- ☐ **2.** What are your concerns about this person becoming your manager? What do you want most from them?
- ☐ **3.** What can the new manager do to motivate the team and help everyone be as productive as possible?
- ☐ **4.** What are the major challenges the manager will face over the next 12 months? (Rank them.)
- ☐ **5.** What are the key relationships that will have to be managed over the next 12 months?
- ☐ **6.** What can this team do to make itself more effective?
- ☐ **7.** What can this team do to make the manager more effective?
- ☐ **8.** What recommendations do you have for how the manager should meet these challenges?
- ☐ **9.** What else should be discussed?

Chapter 4: Map the People Who Matter

Four tools to see and build your stakeholder relationships: a way to map your network, a worksheet to list them, interview questions, and a relationship plan.

4.1 Stakeholder Analysis Checklist

- ☐ **Prepare:** gather any background on your stakeholders and the org charts for your position.
- ☐ **Read the chart, then look past it:** it shows formal roles and reporting lines, but most of the interactions that decide your success are not on it.
- ☐ **Sketch your real network:** beyond your supervisor and direct reports, include other managers, significant peers, relationships that cross reporting lines, others in your in-company network, and your external network (partners, suppliers, clients, customers).

4.2 Stakeholder Analysis Worksheet

List the people in each group, with a note on who they are and why they matter.

Stakeholder group	Names and notes
Immediate supervisor	
Other managers	
Peers and colleagues	
Direct reports	
In-company network	
External network (partners, suppliers, clients, regulators)	
Potential stakeholders (people you need on board)	

Once you have listed them, the companion workbook includes an influence-and-support map that sorts these stakeholders by how much they affect your work and how supportive they are today, so you can see where to spend your attention first.

4.3 Stakeholder Relationship Research Checklist

Before each stakeholder conversation, think through:

- □ Why does this relationship matter to my Key Few Objectives?
- □ How might this person help or hinder them, and what stake do they have in my success?
- □ What questions might they have about my role, and what do I want to learn about theirs?
- □ Where might we agree or conflict, and how will I raise it?

In the conversation, ask about:

- □ Their most critical business issues and key challenges over the next year or two.
- □ Their short- and long-term goals.
- □ The support they want from you and your team.
- □ How you can best learn about their part of the organization.
- □ How your two groups can work best together, and what has worked well before.

4.4 Stakeholder Relationship Plan

Capture the state of each key relationship and your next move, so relationship-building stays deliberate.

Stakeholder	Work needed (expand / repair / create)	Desired outcome	Next actions

Chapter 5: See Resistance Coming

One tool: a checklist for recognizing resistance and planning a constructive response.

5.1 Understanding Resistance Checklist

Spot the four forms of resistance

- ☐ **Lack of communication:** they stop keeping you in the loop or discussing issues openly.
- ☐ **Lack of support:** foot-dragging on the initiatives you are trying to move.
- ☐ **Counterproductive criticism:** reliably critical of you and your ideas.
- ☐ **Passive-aggressive behavior:** agreeing to do something, then not doing it.

Consider where it is coming from

- ☐ Someone who wanted your role and did not get it.
- ☐ Someone with a genuinely difficult working style.
- ☐ Someone anxious about the change you represent. (Resistance is often a natural response to the stress of change.)

If it is a passed-over candidate

- ☐ Ask your boss early who the likely resisters are, and for advice on each.
- ☐ Meet the person in your first weeks, before resentment sets.
- ☐ If they are staying: acknowledge their value, say you are counting on them, commit to their growth, and consider a career conversation.
- ☐ If they are leaving: be candid and empathetic.

The listening-first conversation

- ☐ **1.** Name the specific roadblock you have observed, without criticizing the person.
- ☐ **2.** Ask how they see the situation.

- ☐ **3.** Invite their concerns, and what they would like done differently.
- ☐ **4.** Share your perspective, describing the impact of the behavior, not judging the person.
- ☐ **5.** Define the positive behavior you need, and be clear about expectations.
- ☐ **6.** Tell them, and mean it, that you want them on the team.

If it becomes habitual

- ☐ Consult HR and learn your organization's positive-discipline process.
- ☐ Give the person every reasonable chance to change.
- ☐ Make a decision by eight to ten months in; do not let it drift.
- ☐ Afterward, debrief with HR or your supervisor, and follow through on any career-development commitments.

Chapter 6: Earn Credibility Fast

One tool: a short checklist for taking stock of your credibility and planning how to build it.

6.1 Credibility Research Checklist

Ask yourself

- ☐ With whom do I need to build credibility immediately?
- ☐ Which credibility-building strategies feel most natural for me to use?
- ☐ Is there a highly visible way to secure an early win, to over-deliver for the organization?
- ☐ How can I find out what behavior is expected in a given situation?
- ☐ Who could act as a cultural "interpreter," helping me read events in the context of my new organization?

A quick self-check on the four sources of trust

Rate yourself honestly, and note one action to strengthen the weakest.

- ☐ **Consistency:** do my actions match my words, and do I keep my commitments?
- ☐ **Shared perspective:** do I look for genuine common ground with people?
- ☐ **Frequency:** am I present and interacting, not hiding behind email?
- ☐ **Appropriateness:** do I behave in ways that fit what the people around me expect?

Chapter 7: Understand How Change Works

One tool: a checklist for building the case for a change and thinking through its impact before you take it to your team.

7.1 Supporting Change Research Checklist

- □ What are you seeking to change? What vision, objectives, and business realities are driving it?
- □ What are the losses associated with the change, and how can people be supported through them?
- □ What are the costs of not changing? (An important part of making the case.)
- □ What is the future state the change is meant to bring about? What resources and behaviors will get you there?
- □ What short-term success can the group achieve to gain buy-in and build momentum?
- □ Are there unique opportunities in the change that may not be obvious to the group yet?
- □ What else needs to happen for people to own the change and commit to achieving it?

Chapter 8: Know Yourself

One tool, used three ways: the Success Factors Evaluation. First rate your current self below. Then have three or four trusted people rate you on the same items (Others' Ratings). Then rate your desired self, the version the role needs. The gap between your view and theirs shows your blind spots; the gap between current and desired is your development agenda.

> **DIRECTIONS**
> For each item, mark how descriptive it is of you right now: Most, Somewhat, or Least. It can help to begin each with "I am" or "I." Be honest rather than aspirational; the point is an accurate picture, not a flattering one.

8.1 Success Factors Evaluation

Attribute	Most	Some-what	Least
Social skills and team orientation			
Optimistic			
Cheerful			
Friendly			
Reserved / keep things inside			
Diplomatic			
Team oriented			
Cooperative / help others			
Serious			
Trust others			
Share the credit with others			
Politically savvy			
Hard time saying no to requests			
Communicating and listening			
Good oral communication			

Attribute	Most	Some-what	Least
Good written communication			
Defensive when receiving feedback			
Assertive			
Complain			
Stubborn about viewpoints			
Criticize others			
Good listener			
Persuasive			
Forceful about own desires			
Intellectual and conceptual abilities			
Cautious when making decisions			
Risk taker			
Attentive to details			
Demonstrate good judgment			
Creative			
Effectively analyze problems			
Leading, directing, and developing others			
Good manager of people			
Able to inspire and motivate			
Prefer leading to following			
Help others learn and develop			
Give objective feedback			
Acknowledge and recognize others			
Delegate work			
Take charge			
Hold others accountable			
Planning and organizing			
Good time manager			
Perfectionist			

Attribute	Most	Some-what	Least
Able to set priorities			
Organized			
Plan ahead			
Meet deadlines			
Can do two or more things at once			
Work orientation and effort			
Energetic			
Self motivated			
Dependable			
Agreeable			
Volunteer for assignments			
Pride in the organization			
Personal investment and emotional maturity			
Easily annoyed and irritated			
Flexible and adaptable			
Easily frustrated			
Can handle stress			
Calm in a crisis			
Impatient with others			
Likes reassurance			
Self confident			
Worrier			
Dissatisfied with my work			
Self-knowledge and understanding others			
High personal standards			
Aware of my own limitations			
Overly self critical			
Sensitive to others' feelings			
Tolerant of others			

Chapter 9: Play to Your Strengths

Four tools for leading from your strengths while watching their shadow: a map of how strengths overshoot, a list of common derailers, a development checklist, and a personal audit.

9.1 Potential Drawbacks of Key Strengths

Find your strengths on the left. The right column is what each becomes when overused or used in the wrong situation. Circle the ones most likely to be your shadow in this role.

Key strength	What it becomes when overused
Business intelligence	
Analytic thinker	Analysis paralysis; indecisive; builds overly large staffs.
Decisive	Impulsive or reckless; seen as dictatorial or insensitive to others.
Detail-oriented	Lacks vision and strategic ability.
Highly intelligent	Dismissive of others; intimidating or arrogant; impatient with practical detail.
Innovative	Unrealistic or impractical; wastes time and money.
Prudent	Overly cautious or inflexible; unable to innovate.
Visionary	Insufficient detail, focus, or tactical skill.
Leadership	
Action bias	Reckless and dictatorial, or seen that way.
Charismatic	Deflects healthy skepticism.
Results-oriented	Allows ethical lapses; creates work-life imbalance for self and team.
Sets high standards	Overly selective; never fills positions.
Supportive	Fosters dependence; fails to challenge staff.
Interpersonal and organizational	
Charming	Seen as manipulative; blind to others' perspectives.
Frank	Insensitive; damages important relationships.
Interpersonally skilled	Unwilling to make tough, unpopular decisions.
Team player	Overly risk-averse; fails to assert independent judgment.
Tough negotiator	Unnecessarily damages relationships.
Personal performance	

Key strength	What it becomes when overused
Ambitious	More committed to own advancement than the work; ethical lapses.
Confident	Seen as arrogant; over-commits and under-delivers; resists feedback.
Conscientious	Over-manages; fails to empower and develop others.
Independent	Unable to collaborate.
Principled	Seen as rigid or self-righteous; imposes own values.
Successful track record	Over-reliant on past approaches; arrogant; underestimates new challenges.
Tough	Seen as abrasive; damages relationships.

9.2 Common Derailers to Watch For

Behaviors that reliably send careers off the tracks, especially under pressure. They are usually invisible to the person doing them.

- □ **Arrogant:** thinks they have the only right answer; devalues others' ideas.
- □ **Defensive:** not open to feedback; denies mistakes; blames others.
- □ **Insensitive to others:** abrasive or intimidating, especially under pressure.
- □ **Not trustworthy:** poor follow-through; says one thing, does another.
- □ **Over-manages:** over-controls and meddles; does not empower or develop others.
- □ **Fosters dependence:** never lets people fail; does not delegate.
- □ **Fails to build a team:** treats reports as individuals; does not resolve conflict or build spirit.
- □ **Deploys talent too cautiously:** holds good people back by always playing it safe.
- □ **Does not think strategically:** mired in tactics and detail; lacks broad perspective.

9.3 Strengths and Derailers Checklist

- □ What are the must-have skills for this role?
- □ Which of your strengths should you leverage most here?
- □ Which previous strengths could be viewed as weaknesses in this role or culture?
- □ How might your strengths be overused or turn into weaknesses here?
- □ What adjustments to your style does this situation call for?
- □ What development resources and role models exist in the organization to help?

9.4 Personal Audit Sheet

1. Roles, projects, or relationships that have and have NOT gone well in your career

2. The pattern you see in the situations that have not gone well

3. The strengths or deficits behind your past successes and mistakes

4. Which of your strengths could derail you if overused or misused here

5. Behaviors to practice and skills to build in this role (add to your action plan)

Chapter 10: Manage Up

One tool: questions to help you read your boss's style and adapt to it. Note your answers, then confirm the important ones in a direct conversation.

10.1 Supervisor Style Research Checklist

Style overview

- ☐ What are your boss's preferences on distance, deference, and divergence, and how, specifically, can you accommodate them?
- ☐ What other style preferences do they have? Interruptions welcome or not? Joint brainstorming or solo reflection?

Communication

- ☐ What information does your boss need to receive, and what do they want to be copied on?
- ☐ What are their priorities, and what is most urgent?
- ☐ In what formats do they like different kinds of information (in person, email, voicemail, formal report)?
- ☐ How much detail do they want, concise summaries or full accounts?
- ☐ When and how often do they want updates?

Stresses, pressures, needs

- ☐ What are your boss's most urgent needs? What keeps them up at night?
- ☐ What is most important to thcm?

Support needed

- ☐ Beyond your explicit objectives, how can you best support your boss, as team motivator, as the one who keeps the group focused, as a devil's advocate, or as a bridge-builder with other departments?

Chapter 11: Learn Faster

One tool: an inventory of ways to learn, grouped by the three strategies. Check the ones you already use. You will probably find them clustered in one column. Then circle a few from your under-used strategies to add.

11.1 Learning Techniques Inventory

Learning through people

- □ Debrief with your predecessor.
- □ Use sounding boards, focus groups, interviews, or brainstorming.
- □ Use an assessment checklist to get to know others.
- □ Solve a problem collaboratively.
- □ Work with a coach or a mentor.
- □ Become a mentor to someone else.
- □ Teach someone else what you are learning.
- □ Learn from administrative and support staff.
- □ Join a cross-functional team.
- □ People-watch: observe how people actually operate.
- □ Create a small tradition (for example, team breakfasts).

Learning through material

- □ Review the annual report.
- □ Access and review analyst reports.
- □ Read past and current memos from management.
- □ Study colleagues' business or project plans.
- □ Read business publications (for example, the Wall Street Journal or Forbes).
- □ Subscribe to relevant periodicals or newsletters.
- □ Observe organizational symbols (awards on walls, lobby displays).
- □ Read the organization's mission and vision statements.

- ☐ Explore the intranet.
- ☐ Review project files.

Learning through doing

- ☐ Take tours of other areas.
- ☐ Record meetings where appropriate, and review them.
- ☐ Debrief yourself after key events.
- ☐ Vary your meeting settings (try an offsite).
- ☐ Vary your meeting approach (use a facilitator or a note-taker).
- ☐ Conduct a small study or pilot.
- ☐ Use shared calendars to see how time and attention flow.
- ☐ Volunteer for a company or unit initiative.
- ☐ Map out your unit's process flow.

Chapter 12: Read the Culture

One tool: questions to help you decode how your organization really works. Work through them with your local guides, your boss, a savvy peer, someone in HR, rather than trying to answer them alone.

12.1 Organizational Politics and Culture Research Checklist

The politics: how power works

- ☐ How are decisions really made, and what influencing approach works best (collaboration, negotiation, persuasion)?
- ☐ Who are the formal and informal leaders, the key players?
- ☐ Who are the influencers and opinion leaders, the people who really get things done?
- ☐ Whose support is needed to shape a significant initiative, and where are the pockets of power?
- ☐ Is the organization centralized or decentralized, and how much power sits at the corporate offices?

The culture: the unwritten rules and values

- ☐ How do people get things done, through the formal chain of command or informal networks?
- ☐ How does your boss's manager make decisions and get things done?
- ☐ How does the organization communicate, and what is the most effective way to be heard?
- ☐ Are top-level managers visible and accessible?
- ☐ Does the organization take a short-term or long-term perspective?
- ☐ How are inconsistencies in performance dealt with? Are they tolerated?
- ☐ Are people rewarded for thinking outside the box?

- ☐ How are differences of opinion handled, openly, offline, or not at all?
- ☐ What are the social traditions and norms (holiday gifts, social events), and how do they affect the business?
- ☐ What are the landmark moments, stories, or legends that serve as touchstones for people?
- ☐ What does the organization truly value, creativity, risk-taking, loyalty, harmony, quality, efficiency?

Chapter 13: Learn How Work Gets Done

One tool: questions to help you understand the organization's structure and the business systems that carry work into and out of your team.

13.1 Business Systems Research Checklist

- ☐ What is the structure of the organization, and where does your team sit in the flow of work?
- ☐ Which key business processes and policies do your objectives depend on, and how does each actually run (including timing)?

  Common processes to scan: sales and service delivery; new product development; financial cycles (operating and capital budgets); HR (hiring, performance reviews, compensation, succession); administration (purchasing, expenditures); technology (standards, information security).
- ☐ What is the competition doing, and how does your organization compare?
- ☐ How current is the organization technologically? How well is your team trained on it, and how do you access training funds?
- ☐ What are the benefits and drawbacks of the compensation structure for your business unit?
- ☐ What external affiliations and resources (industry bodies, research firms) are available, and how can you leverage them?

Chapter 14: Size Up Your Team

One tool, used once per competency your objectives require: the Team Competency Gap Analysis. Name the competency, tie it to the objective it serves, then break it into observable behaviors and mark which your team already has and which are gaps.

14.1 Team Competency Gap Analysis (template)

Competency *The knowledge, skill, or ability being assessed.*	

Key Few Objective(s) it advances *Which of your KFOs this competency helps deliver.*	

Vision element(s) it supports *How it connects to where you are taking the team.*	

Break the competency into component behaviors, then mark each.

Component behavior needed	Exists?	A gap?
1.		
2.		
3.		
4.		
5.		
6.		

14.2 A Completed Example

Competency	

- Self-service knowledge management.

Key Few Objective advanced

- Launch a self-service knowledge base for the top 20 issues, deflecting 15 percent of tickets by end of Q2.

Component behavior needed	Exists?	A gap?
1. Team logs the root causes of recurring issues	Yes	
2. Team reviews ticket trends monthly to spot top issues	Yes	
3. Team writes clear, customer-facing help articles		Gap
4. Someone owns and maintains the knowledge base		Gap
5. Team measures deflection (tickets avoided)		Gap

Read-out: *the raw material is there (the team already sees the patterns), but three behaviors are missing. The plan writes itself: develop the writing skill, assign an owner, and add a deflection metric.*

Chapter 15: Navigate Competing Agendas

Two tools: a checklist that walks a conflict from anticipation to resolution, and a form for bringing a challenge to your advisory board.

15.1 Conflicting Agenda Checklist

Anticipating conflict

- ☐ How will others be affected by your initiative, and what do they stand to lose? Follow the consequences downstream.
- ☐ When similar things were tried before, what negative reactions came up, and what was the impact?
- ☐ Which people or coalitions might resist, and in what form?

Clarifying agendas: conflict and alignment

- ☐ What is getting in the way of mutual support?
- ☐ What is your perspective, and your must-haves? What are your counterpart's?
- ☐ How does your perspective differ from theirs?
- ☐ What goals do you share that you could work on together?
- ☐ What is the real basis of the conflict (competition for resources, difference in philosophy, disagreement about how to operate)?

Finding a solution

- ☐ If a solution met both parties' needs, what would it look like?
- ☐ What do you each need from the other for your common goals?
- ☐ What are alternative ways you can each get what you need?
- ☐ What criteria should decide a solution that works for both?

Moving forward

- ☐ How will you make sure the solution works for both of you?
- ☐ What barriers could you face, and how will you overcome them?
- ☐ How will you support each other going forward?

15.2 Challenge Consultation Form

Use this to bring a specific challenge to a member of your advisory board.

Challenge (briefly summarize) and the advisor to consult

Desired result

Actions agreed upon with your advisor

How you will measure progress

Resources needed

Initial steps

Chapter 16: Build an Inclusive Team

One tool, in two parts: reflective questions about inclusion, and a set of everyday moves that build psychological safety.

16.1 Inclusive Culture Checklist

Reflect on inclusion

- □ Is difference visible on your team, or does nearly everyone look, act, talk, and think alike?
- □ Are people comfortable talking about differences? What could you do to open a healthy, ongoing dialogue?
- □ How has diversity already been leveraged on your team or in the organization, and how can you build on it?
- □ What history underlies your team's reactions to difference?
- □ What current best practices around inclusion could you bring into your area?

Build psychological safety (everyday moves)

- □ Invite dissent explicitly ("what am I missing?") and thank whoever offers it.
- □ Admit your own mistakes and uncertainty out loud.
- □ Make sure the quiet voices are heard, call on people or ask for input in writing.
- □ Respond to bad news and errors with curiosity, not blame.
- □ Notice who is overloaded, left out, or has gone quiet, and act on it.

Chapter 17: Craft a Vision Worth Following

Three checklists for the three steps of building a vision: gather information, analyze it, then design the picture.

17.1 Vision Gathering Checklist

Go wide: who to talk to

- □ Your team, your peers, and your boss.
- □ Customers, suppliers, and other associates.
- □ People who usually disagree with you.
- □ Fresh-eyed newcomers, and seasoned strategists.
- □ Mavericks and unconventional thinkers.

What to ask about

- □ Your unit's environment: clients, competition, external factors, position in the market.
- □ Your unit's current role and unique contribution within the organization.
- □ How your unit is perceived inside the organization, and how the organization is perceived outside.
- □ Your key stakeholders and their needs, and the competing options they have.
- □ Where your industry stands, and where markets and global developments are heading.
- □ Go deep: the organization's overarching mission, vision, and values (yours must align).

17.2 Vision Analysis Checklist (SWOT)

Strengths and opportunities

- □ What are your team's key strengths, and how can you leverage them?
- □ Where can your team make its greatest contribution?
- □ What opportunities can you capitalize on?

- ☐ What are your key success factors and capabilities, and what do customers value most?

Weaknesses and threats

- ☐ What are your weaknesses, and how can you mitigate them?
- ☐ What events could hit you hard, and how would you avert or even capitalize on them?
- ☐ What threats to your effectiveness need managing?
- ☐ What do customers dislike, and how can you fix it?

17.3 Vision Design Checklist

Given what you gathered and analyzed:

- ☐ What should your team focus on (key services and products)?
- ☐ What unique contribution should it make to the organization's mission, and how do you align to it?
- ☐ Who should its customers be in the future?
- ☐ What vision would energize your current team and attract the talent you want?
- ☐ What role should technology play?
- ☐ What should the team do better, what should it start, and what should it stop?
- ☐ What culture do you need to build, and how should performance be measured?

Chapter 18: Win Commitment to the Vision

Three tools for turning your vision into the team's: moves that build support, a way to diagnose resistance, and a guide to running a visioning meeting.

18.1 Vision Support-Building Checklist

- ☐ Involve key stakeholders and decision-makers in shaping the vision; invite their reservations early, and process their input before you crystallize your thinking.
- ☐ Build in early wins that are strategically linked to the vision and help the wider organization, then celebrate them so people see real results.
- ☐ Identify the influence networks and opinion leaders, and collaborate with them to champion the vision.
- ☐ Educate and inspire people around the vision: find ways to communicate it, and make it compelling.

18.2 Vision Resistance Checklist

When you hit resistance, find its source.

Negative past experience

- ☐ What experience have people had with similar initiatives before?
- ☐ If it was negative, was the problem the idea, the way it was implemented, or the person behind it?
- ☐ What was the longer-term impact, positive, negative, or none?

Lack of control or input

- ☐ Have you sought enough reaction and input from the people affected?
- ☐ Do people feel out of control? How could they feel more in control? Are you trying to do too much too soon?

Change itself feels threatening

- ☐ Loss of competence from having to do unfamiliar things?
- ☐ A clash with someone's personal values?

- ☐ The plain anxiety of ambiguity, better the devil they know?

18.3 Vision Meeting Facilitation Guide

A live meeting beats a circulated draft: it engages the team with the vision, and shows you mean it.

Set the stage

- ☐ Consider having HR help facilitate, so you are free to listen and people can be candid.
- ☐ Go offsite to avoid interruptions, in a flexible space with room for break-outs.
- ☐ Have your direct reports lead segments of the agenda.
- ☐ Commit each sub-team to drafting what the vision means for them and their next steps.

Facilitation guidelines

- ☐ Keep your own speaking time short; your role in this meeting is to listen.
- ☐ Break the larger group into smaller groups to get candid feedback.

Chapter 19: Lead a Team You Rarely See

One tool in two parts: an agreement your team writes together about how it will work across distance, and a completed example so you can see what a real one looks like before you build your own.

19.1 Distributed Team Working Agreement

Draft your answers, then bring them to the team and settle them together. An agreement you write alone is a policy. An agreement the team writes is a norm.

How we communicate

- ☐ Which channel is for what: what belongs in chat, in email, in a document, on a call?
- ☐ What is our expected response time in each channel, and does it differ after hours?
- ☐ What is explicitly not urgent, so nobody feels obliged to answer at night?
- ☐ How do we raise a problem early, and who do we raise it to?

When we are available

- ☐ What hours do we overlap, and what is protected as focus time?
- ☐ How do we show that we are away, and is it expected or apologized for?
- ☐ Which recurring meetings fall outside someone's normal day, and how do we rotate that cost?

How we meet

- ☐ When anyone is remote, is everyone on their own screen?
- ☐ Cameras: expected, optional, or situational, and have we said so out loud?
- ☐ Who makes sure the quiet voices and the remote voices are heard?
- ☐ What must be circulated before a meeting for it to be worth holding?

How decisions get recorded

- ☐ Where does a decision live once it is made, and who writes it down?
- ☐ Do we capture the reasoning, not just the outcome?
- ☐ How does someone who missed the conversation catch up without asking?

How we stay connected

- ☐ How does someone new to the team meet everyone, not just their nearest colleagues?
- ☐ What is our deliberate substitute for the unplanned conversation?
- ☐ How would we notice if someone had gone quiet, and whose job is it to notice?
- ☐ When do we get in the same room, and what is that time reserved for?

19.2 A Completed Example

Elena's team of nine, across three cities and two time zones.

How we communicate. Chat for anything needed within the day. Email for anything that needs a record but not a discussion. A document for anything a person outside the conversation will need to understand later. A call for anything with feeling attached to it. Chat within four working hours, email within one working day, nothing expected after 6 p.m. local or on weekends. If something is genuinely urgent, phone the person; if you would not phone them, it is not urgent.

When we are available. Core overlap is 10 a.m. to 2 p.m. Central, and we keep it clear of recurring meetings so it stays usable. Tuesday and Thursday mornings are protected focus time for everyone. Calendars are honest, and being away needs no explanation. The Monday team call rotates between 9 a.m. and 11 a.m. Central each quarter so the same two people are not always the ones getting up early.

How we meet. If one person is remote, everyone joins from their own screen. Cameras on for one-on-ones and for anything difficult, optional for working sessions. Whoever is running the meeting is responsible for making sure everyone has spoken before a decision lands. No agenda circulated by the day before means the meeting is canceled, not held anyway.

How decisions get recorded. Every decision goes in the team decision log within a day, written by whoever ran the meeting, in three lines: what we decided, why, and what we considered instead. Anyone can read the log and be current in ten minutes without asking a colleague to re-explain.

How we stay connected. New joiners get a thirty-minute call with every person on the team in their first two weeks, scheduled for them rather than left to their initiative. Every Friday one person shares something they are working on for ten minutes, whether it went well or not. Elena reviews her one-on-one coverage monthly and reaches out first to whoever she has seen least. The whole team is in one room twice a year, and that time is spent on the things that are genuinely hard to do at a distance: planning, disagreement, and lunch.

Chapter 20: Deepen the Relationships That Carry You

Two tools: a maintenance check to take the temperature of each key relationship, and an enhancement-and-repair checklist to act on what you find. Both are good to work through with your team.

20.1 Relationship Maintenance Checklist

- ☐ Does this relationship need repairing in any way?
- ☐ For each new relationship, what kind of start have you gotten off to?
- ☐ What potential strains might you not have seen at first?
- ☐ What style differences have you noticed, and how can you accommodate them?
- ☐ On a scale of 1 to 10, how strong was this relationship when you started, and how strong is it now?
- ☐ What specific enhancement or repair actions should go into your action plan?

20.2 Relationship Enhancement Checklist

Enhancing a strong relationship

- ☐ How would enhancing this relationship improve both units' effectiveness?
- ☐ Where could you improve the efficiencies between your two units?
- ☐ What barriers exist, and how can you remove them together?
- ☐ How can you leverage each other's talents, and what can you learn from each other?
- ☐ Who should be involved in strengthening the relationship?

Repairing a damaged relationship

- ☐ How was the relationship damaged, what is the history, and who was involved?
- ☐ What is at the core, lack of trust, conflicting agendas, credibility, something else?

- ☐ What is the damage costing the business (lost productivity, missed synergies, lower quality)?
- ☐ Who needs to be involved in repairing it?
- ☐ How might you repair it, take ownership of your part, open communication about differences, use HR or an outside mediator, and agree on better communication going forward?

Chapter 21: Lock In Support for the Long Haul

One tool: a checklist for closing the organizational gaps that make a vision hard to execute, and hard to keep support behind. (For building support and handling resistance directly, the Vision Support-Building and Vision Resistance Checklists in the Chapter 18 section also apply.)

21.1 Closing the Gaps Strategy Checklist

Skill gap

- ☐ Can existing team members build the skills through coaching, training, or developmental assignments?
- ☐ Do you need to add or replace members, contract for services, or bring in consultation?
- ☐ Do you need to redefine, create, or eliminate positions?

Knowledge gap

- ☐ Can existing members gain the knowledge through research, coaching, or training?
- ☐ Do you need to add or replace members, contract, or bring in consultation?

Motivation gap

- ☐ Which need to change to pull the team toward the vision: leadership approach, performance expectations, incentives, or other policies?

Resource gap

- ☐ What additional resources are needed, and how will you acquire them, short term and long term?

Policy and process gap

- ☐ Are policies fully aligned with your vision and Key Few Objectives?
- ☐ What policies or processes hinder your objectives (compensation, succession, allocation of development resources), and how can they be corrected?

Values gap

- ☐ What do you need to do to make the new values clear, and how will you model them yourself?

Chapter 22: Measure Progress and Plan What's Next

Two tools: a progress evaluation to take honest stock (the same questions, answered from three perspectives, your own, your supervisor's, and HR's), and a roadmap for planning what comes next.

22.1 Progress Evaluation (Self)

- ☐ Have you worked through all 22 chapters?
- ☐ Do you have good agreement with your boss and key stakeholders on your Role Charter?
- ☐ Do your Role Charter or Key Few Objectives need updating now?
- ☐ How much progress have you made on each Key Few Objective?
- ☐ How well are you executing your action plan?
- ☐ Have you attended to each of the focus areas, and which most needs more attention now?
- ☐ Have you identified and recruited your personal advisory board?
- ☐ What are your most important strengths at this point?
- ☐ Where is it most important for you to keep developing or change behavior?

Have your boss (and, if useful, HR) answer the same questions, then compare. The gaps between your view and theirs are where the real learning is.

22.2 Roadmap for Continued Success

Turn the evaluation into a plan for your next phase. Consult your advisory board as you fill it in.

Objectives for your next phase (your updated Key Few Objectives)

Skills to keep building

Relationships to keep tending

Advisory board members to consult, and on what

Next steps, with dates

BACK MATTER

Notes

Sources and Further Reading

Sources for the research findings referenced in the book, listed by chapter. Everything not cited here draws on the author's twenty years of consulting practice.

Introduction: managers who receive no training. The finding that the large majority of new managers step into the role untrained comes from the Chartered Management Institute's Good Management Report (CMI and YouGov, 2023), a survey of 4,500 UK workers and managers: 82 percent of those entering management roles had received no formal management or leadership training, a group CMI calls accidental managers.

Chapter 3: the manager assimilation meeting. The structured assimilation session described here descends from the New Manager Assimilation process developed at General Electric, since adapted by HR teams across many industries.

Chapter 6: credibility equals trustworthiness plus expertise. The two-factor view of credibility traces to the Yale persuasion studies: Carl Hovland, Irving Janis, and Harold Kelley, Communication and Persuasion (Yale University Press, 1953). Persuasion research in the decades since has repeatedly found that audiences weigh a source's trustworthiness at least as heavily as its expertise.

Chapter 8: the gap between how we see ourselves and how others see us. Tasha Eurich's multi-year research program found that while 95 percent of people believe they are self-aware, only 10 to 15 percent actually are. See Tasha Eurich, Insight (Crown, 2017), and her Harvard Business Review article "What Self-Awareness Really Is (and How to Cultivate It)" (January 2018).

Chapter 9: derailers. The research on why successful careers go off the tracks began with Morgan McCall and Michael Lombardo, "Off the Track: Why and How Successful Executives Get Derailed" (Center for Creative Leadership, 1983), and continues in Robert Hogan and Joyce Hogan's work on the dark side of personality, the basis of the Hogan Development Survey. The pattern of strengths overused becoming weaknesses runs throughout both.

Chapter 10: the relationship with your boss. Gallup's State of the American Manager (2015) found that managers account for at least 70 percent of the variance in team engagement across business units, and that roughly one in two US employees has left a job to get away from a manager at some point in their career. Few single factors shape your working life, or your team's, as much as this relationship.

Chapter 16: psychological safety as the top predictor of team performance. The concept and the core evidence come from Amy Edmondson, beginning with "Psychological Safety and Learning Behavior in Work Teams," Administrative Science Quarterly 44 (1999), and developed in The Fearless Organization (Wiley, 2019). Google's Project Aristotle, an internal study of more than 180 of its own teams, reached the same conclusion at corporate scale: psychological safety was the strongest of five predictors of team effectiveness, well ahead of who was on the team. See Charles Duhigg, "What Google Learned From Its Quest to Build the Perfect Team," New York Times Magazine, February 25, 2016, and Google's re:Work guide to team effectiveness.

Chapter 16: diverse and inclusive teams perform better. Boston Consulting Group found that companies with above-average diversity on their leadership teams reported 19 percent higher innovation revenue than those below average: Rocio Lorenzo and colleagues, "How Diverse and Inclusive Leadership Teams Boost Innovation" (BCG, 2018). McKinsey's Diversity Wins (2020) found top-quartile executive-team diversity associated with a significantly higher likelihood of financial outperformance.

Chapter 19: the people you see get more of you. Two lines of research converge here. Kimberly Elsbach and Daniel Cable's work on passive face time, the amount of time a person is simply observed at work without interacting, found that being seen produces spontaneous trait inferences: presence during normal hours reads as dependable, and presence outside normal hours reads as committed, whether or not the employee has demonstrated either quality. See Kimberly D. Elsbach, Daniel M. Cable, and Jeffrey W. Sherman, "How Passive Face Time Affects Perceptions of Employees: Evidence of Spontaneous Trait Inference," Human Relations 63 (2010), and Elsbach and Cable, "Why Showing Your Face at Work Matters," MIT Sloan Management Review (Summer 2012). The career consequence shows up in the best-known field experiment on remote work, run at the Chinese travel company Ctrip, where call center employees randomly assigned to work from home were 13 percent more productive and left the company at half the rate of their office-based colleagues, yet were promoted less often at the same level of measured performance: Nicholas Bloom, James Liang, John Roberts, and Zhichun Jenny Ying, "Does Working from Home Work? Evidence from a Chinese Experiment," Quarterly Journal of Economics 130, no. 1 (2015).

About the Author

Jesse Jacoby is the founder and principal of Emergent, a Denver-based consultancy specializing in organizational change, leadership transitions, and helping new leaders succeed. For more than two decades he has worked alongside managers and executives, from first-time supervisors to senior leaders, at Fortune 500 companies such as PepsiCo, Gap Inc., Walgreens, and Lowe's, as well as mid-sized firms and fast-growing startups.

The programs Jesse has designed have helped thousands of managers step into leadership with confidence. He is also the architect of methodologies that help companies assess and activate AI opportunities across their workforce, the same human-plus-AI partnership this book teaches new managers to build.

Jesse holds an MBA from Johns Hopkins University and a master's degree in communications. He writes and speaks on leadership, management, and change. Find him at EmergentConsultants.com;

the tools from this book, and the companion workbook, live at TheEmergentManager.com.

Keep Going

The Free Starter Kit

The tools in this book work harder when you can fill them in, save them, and come back to them. The Free Starter Kit gives you editable versions of the core tools, plus a short walkthrough of the first thirty days.

TheEmergentManager.com

If this book helped, a short review helps another new manager find it.

Made in the USA
Coppell, TX
26 August 2026

86953724R00114